A Mini-Encyclopaedia of

CHINESE CRAFTS

A Mini-Encyclopaedia of

CHINESE CRAFTS

Roberta Helmer Stalberg
Ruth Nesi

TIMES BOOKS
International

ACKNOWLEDGMENTS

We wish to express our gratitude to Mr. Chu Chen-kuang for his fine line drawings and assistance with many details. We would also like to thank the Guangxi Arts and Crafts Research Institute, the Yunnan Arts and Crafts Research Institute, and the New York delegation of China's National Arts and Crafts Import and Export Corporation. Thanks to Nancy Lyon, Helen Rosen, Esther Gollobin, Norma and Howard Hyman, Helen Reeve, and Rewi Alley for their assistance, and to Maxwell Hearn for reading the manuscript and giving excellent critical and constructive advice. Ruth wishes to express special gratitude to all her colleagues at Sunweave Linen. A final note of thanks is due to Jim and Christopher for their continuing support.

—The Authors

First published in 1980 by Eurasia Press as *China's Crafts.*
This edition published by Times Books International.

TIMES CENTRE
1 New Industrial Road
Singapore 1953

With appreciation to Tangs Superstore for the loan of their Chinese crafts for cover photography.

Printed by Khai Wah Litho, Singapore

CONTENTS

PREFACE

Nor less the coarser household wares,
The willow pattern, that we knew
In childhood, with its bridge of blue
Leading to unknown thoroughfares;
The solitary man who stares
At the white river flowing through
Its arches, the fantastic trees
And wild perspective of the view;
And intermingled among these
The tiles that in our nurseries
Filled us with wonder and delight,
Or haunted us in dreams at night . . .

"KERAMOS," *1877*
Henry Wadsworth Longfellow

Many Americans and Europeans got their first glimpse of China from the blue-and-white "willow pattern" porcelains commonly seen in homes since the late eighteenth century. These patterns displayed slender figures atop curving bridges or resting beneath graceful willows. By the mid-nineteenth century, swift clipper ships were carrying vast quantities of Chinese goods to the West, despite the great distances and dangers of the voyage. The ships' holds were filled with lacquer screens, silks, fans, porcelains, and tea, that precious commodity which had provoked a revolution. Western consumers were fascinated with the unusual colors, exotic designs, and exquisite craftsmanship of these wares.

Today there is once again an influx of Chinese arts and crafts, featured in department stores and craft shops in virtually every large European and American city. As in past centuries, examples of fine craftsmanship are available to the knowledgeable buyer with an understanding of China's craft traditions and aesthetic development.

The aim of this book is to provide a broad yet handy guide to the crafts of China. Part One presents the background and heritage of Chinese arts and crafts and their symbols, while Part Two describes specific crafts. Those interested in further reading should consult the lists following each chapter. A shopping guide at the end of the book provides information on current craft production and retail centers in China. Because new Chinese craft outlets are opening every day, however, these guides can provide only a brief introduction to shopping sources, and travelers to China are advised to inquire locally about new outlets. Specialists and students of Chinese may wish to consult the Glossary in order to find Chinese characters; non-simplified characters have been used, in keeping with the prevailing practice in the West. *Pinyin,* the now official Chinese system of romanization, has been adopted, however, as this is increasingly replacing the old Wade-Giles system.

As a final note, we would like to add that almost all the symbols used today in the People's Republic of China have lost their superstitious overtones. Symbols expressing wishes for success under the old feudal system have likewise lost their specific meaning but retain their general sense of a wish for prosperity and good fortune. Today these patterns are valued mainly for their beauty and decorative functions.

RHS and RN

New York
October 1980

INTRODUCTION

I have sweet and bitter memories of old China, where I lived with my parents during the civil war in the later forties. Among the most pleasant times were those Saturday mornings when the curio dealers would come to our home in the Canadian Embassy compound and spread their wondrous wares on the floor of our reception room. Then the whole family would gather to view the display of Chinese *dong-xi,* which consisted of the typical traditional crafts that have been created for over four thousand years. There were jade and silver ornaments, embroidered robes and delicate table cloths, fine porcelains and crude pottery, ceramic grave figures, lacquerware, intricate ivory balls, cloisonné vases and wooden carvings, ginger jars, snuff bottles, scrolls and precious jewelry, as well as fascinating curios of all descriptions.

Crowned jade figurine, Shang dynasty

My favorite curio dealer was a delightful old rogue called Lao Tang. His gray mustache curled slyly around the corners of his mouth and joined the wispy white beard that straggled sparsely over his chest. His loose, black silk pajamas were tattered and his black, red-tassled mandarin cap had lost its shape but to me he looked like a grand wizard as he imperiously commanded his sturdy servant to unwrap the mysterious cloth bags which he had carried to our home on each end of a bamboo *yo* stick. During this laying out ceremony Lao Tang would caution his servant about breakage and gravely remind us all of the great value and rarity of the objects. His grandiose respect enhanced the value of even the lowliest piece and I was convinced I was gazing upon the most priceless treasures in the world and wondered why my father was not similarly impressed. But father had been born and brought up in China and had learned at an early age that bargaining over prices was a fine art in China and had to be carried on with acute finesse in a manner of studied indifference if one expected to obtain any object at a reasonable price. This was in 1947 during the height of inflation in China when the US dollar was worth about 500,000 *yuan* (CNC), so bargaining was carried out in American money.

The ritual my father and Lao Tang performed was almost always the same. Father was careful not to let the dealer know which article he really wanted but instead showed an interest in a piece of junk. Lao Tang would then, as a special favor to an honored guest in China, ask an outrageously high price for it. Father, in turn, would offer a shamefully low bid and the spirited bargaining would begin with both opponents aware that this was only a warming up process. They were careful not to reach an agreement. Finally there would be dramatic sighs and laments from Lao Tang as he bid his servant to wrap up the collection. After a few pieces had been packed the old wizard would look around sorrowfully, stroke his beard and moan about how it grieved him to leave without satisfying the honorable diplomat. We would then implore father to look at some more *dong-xi*. Father would inevitably agree and Lao Tang would happily squat on the floor and begin to ask even more outrageous prices. He was a great actor; he wheedled and lied and flattered while father firmly clung to his reputation as an unyielding skinflint. Time meant nothing to father and Lao Tang as the game of bargaining was being played.

Lacquer box lid, Ming dynasty

One morning Lao Tang brought a small teakwood dressing case bound in silver. I watched wide-eyed as he opened the lid to expose the mirror under it. Inside, preserved in small compartments, were all the appliances of the feminine toilet. One drawer contained the fine white powder the Chinese woman fluffed on their faces after polishing their skin with a hot damp cloth; another held the carmine which tinted the cheeks. There were separate compartments for an ivory comb, a hairbrush, toothbrush, tongue scraper, ear picker, back scratcher, gum to keep the hair in place, jade hair pins, and a variety of gray and black pastes to enhance the eyes. In a secret box, disguised as a false bottom, were two gold filigree fingernail protectors. I was entranced. When Lao Tang was not watching I begged father to get it for me.

After going rather quickly through the preliminary stages of bargaining, and after Lao Tang was about to pack up for the third time, father said to him . . .

"Lao Tang, you are an old man and have gone to so much trouble. I would like to buy something just to please you but your prices are really too high for a poor diplomat to pay."

"But for you I will make a tremendous sacrifice," replied the old man, "but for you alone."

"Well perhaps if that cosmetic case is very cheap I would consider it."

Lao Tang sensed that this was his chance. The words tumbled out. "That case once belonged to the Empress Dowager herself," he lied, "and was brought to Nanking by my third cousin whose mother was a concubine of the Emperor. It was smuggled out of the Imperial palace in Peking by her eunuch. It is the only box of its kind in China, in the world! But you may have it for the ridiculously low price of thirty dollars." He opened his palms to prove that he was being completely honest and smiled charmingly.

"A pity," replied Father, "because that is twenty dollars too much. Oh well, I really don't want it anyway."

"Maybe twenty-eight? As a special favor."

"Twelve."

Lao Tang assumed a posture of hurt dignity. "I would be losing money. Twenty-five?" He sighed loudly and looked at my mother mournfully.

"Fifteen," snapped Father, "last price."

"Twenty?" pleaded the old wizard with tears rolling down his cheeks, "but only on the condition that you tell no one what you paid, ever! It is too ridiculous!"

By now I was on the side of the crafty merchant. "Please Dad, take it."

"Nineteen," father countered weakly.

"All right, all right," sighed Lao Tang wringing his hands, "but please don't let me eat so much bitterness next time."

Father counted out the money carefully and handed it to Lao Tang who presented the box to him with the air of someone parting with the crown jewels. The game was over.

Clay warrior from the tomb of Qin Shi-huang-di

The days of bargaining over prices are long gone but many of China's magnificent crafts, which are so beautifully displayed in this book, are now available at fixed prices in stores in the United States. When I recently returned to China I was pleased to discover that contemporary crafts are being produced in the traditional style with the dedicated care and creativity characteristic of a golden age.

During the wars and turmoil of the first fifty years of the present century, many of China's traditional arts and crafts were lost or neglected. Only in the past two decades has there been a revitalization of the ancient crafts and a new awakening of peasant handicrafts.

In this scholarly and readable book Roberta Stalberg and Ruth Nesi introduce the reader to China's contemporary crafts, chronicle their historical development, and reveal the meaning of the esoteric symbols which decorate many of the artifacts. I think the reader will be entranced by the illustrations and story of these beautiful objects as I was by Lao Tang's teakwood dressing case.

AUDREY TOPPING

Scarsdale, New York
Fall 1980

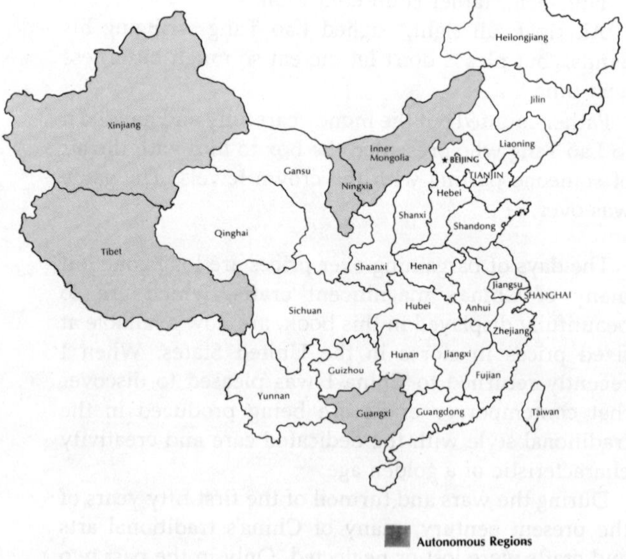

CHINA'S CRAFT CENTERS

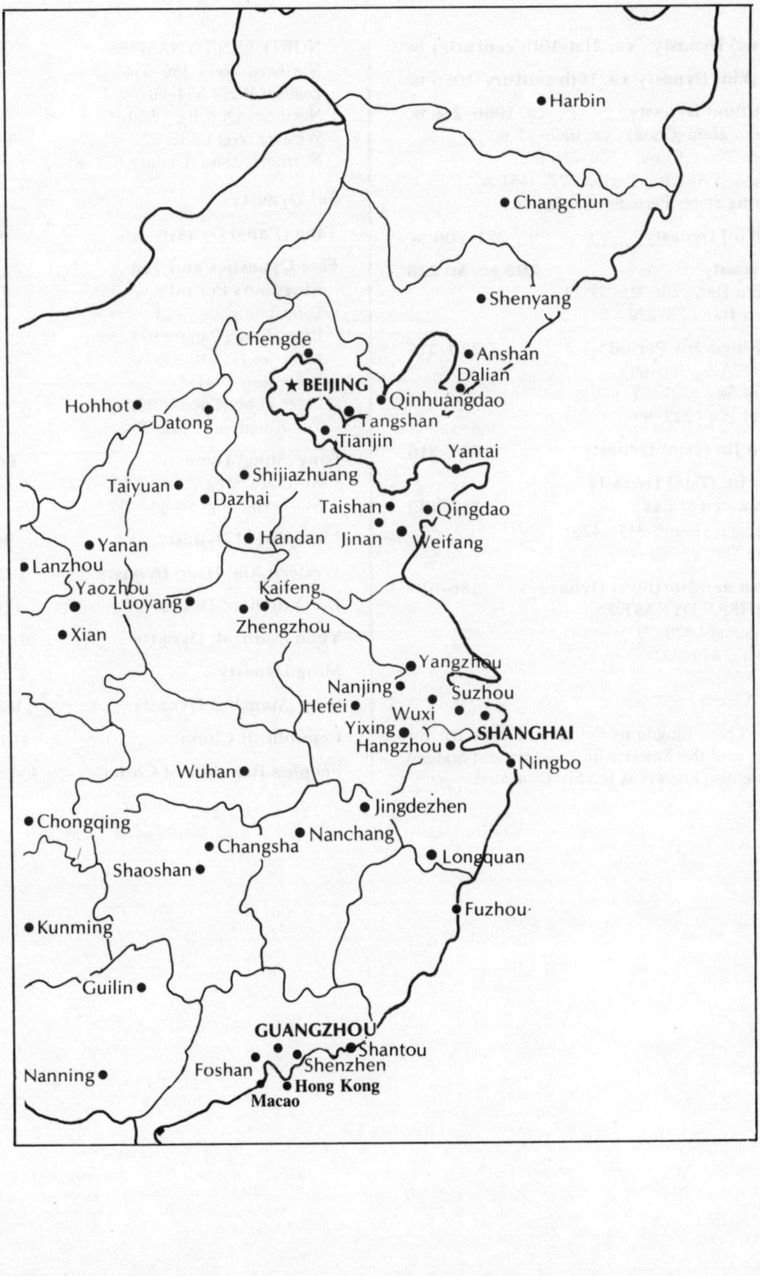

CHRONOLOGY OF CHINESE DYNASTIES

Xia (Hsia) Dynasty ca. 21st-16th centuries BC

Shang (Yin) Dynasty ca. 16th century-1066 BC

Zhou (Chou) Dynasty ca. 1066-256 BC
- Western Zhou (Chou) / ca. 1066-77 BC
- Eastern Zhou (Chou) / 770-256 BC
- Spring and Autumn Period / 772-481 BC
- Warrring States Period / 403-221 BC

Qin (Ch'in) Dynasty 221-206 BC

Han Dynasty 206 BC-AD 220
- Western Han / 206 AD-AD 23
- Eastern Han / 25-220

Three Kingdoms Period* 220-316
- State of Wei / 220-65
- State of Shu / 221-63
- State of Wu / 222-80

Western Jin (Tsin) Dynasty 265-316

Eastern Jin (Tsin) Dynasty and Sixteen States 317-439
- Eastern Jin (Tsin) / 317–420
- Sixteen States / 304-439

Southern and Northern Dynasties 386-581

SOUTHERN DYNASTIES
- Song (Sung) / 420-79
- Qi (Ch'i) / 479-502
- Liang / 502-57
- Chen (Ch'en) / 557-89

NORTHERN DYNASTIES
- Northern Wei / 386-534
- Eastern Wei / 534-50
- Northern Qi (Ch'i) / 550-77
- Western Wei / 535-57
- Northern Zhou (Chou) / 557-81

Sui Dynasty 581-618

Tang (T'ang) Dynasty 618-907

Five Dynasties and Ten Kingdoms Period 907-79
- Later Liang / 907-23
- Later Tang (T'ang) / 923-36
- Later Jin (Tsin) / 936-46
- Later Han / 947-50
- Later Zhou (Chou) / 951-60
- Ten Kingdoms / 902-79

Song (Sung) Dynasty 960-1279
- Northern Song (Sung) / 960-1127
- Southern Song (Sung) / 1127-1279

Liao (Kitan) Dynasty 907-1125

Western Xia (Hsia) Dynasty 1032-1227

Jin (Nurchen) Dynasty 1115-1234

Yuan (Mongol) Dynasty 1279-1368

Ming Dynasty 1368-1644

Qing (Manchu) Dynasty 1644-1911

Republic of China 1912-1949

People's Republic of China Estab. 1949

*The Three Kingdoms Period, the Western Jin Dynasty, and the Eastern Jin Dynasty and Sixteen States are also known as the Six Dynasties.

PART I

THE SETTING

Jade carver and apprentices

CHAPTER 1

THE ARTISANS

Through the steep, layered hills of Shaanxi Province in the central part of northern China, the Yellow River threads its way among desert wastes, mountains of yellow earth punctuated with deep ravines, high plateaux of fertile and wind-blown loess soil to the basin of the Wei River. The Wei Valley is China's cultural birthplace. Amid the natural protection of mountains and plateaux on south, west, and north, China's earliest civilization flowered. Here Neolithic villagers wove their first cloth and decorated their pottery with delicate paintings of fish and animals, magical creatures, and swirling geometric designs.

As civilization advanced, ancient kings of the Shang and Zhou dynasties commanded that huge cauldrons and tripods be cast in bronze, so that they could communicate with their divine ancestors in solemn rituals. They and their noble relatives ate from fine ceramics. They dressed in stately robes of silk and adorned themselves with pendants of jade, mother-of-pearl, and tortoise shell. They hunted and fought in fine chariots with bronze fittings. And when they died, they were buried with these same majestic bronze vessels, weapons, chariots, pottery, and stone carvings which surrounded them in life. Like all ancient peoples, the Chinese believed that objects placed in the tomb would accompany the dead ruler to his new life in the after-

Bronze vessel, Shang dynasty

world. The belief in an afterlife created a tremendous demand for luxury items; hundreds of skilled artisans worked for years to create or replace the objects buried in a single royal tomb.

THE CRAFTSMEN

The craftsmen who made these utensils and decorations almost four thousand years ago were extremely skilled and experienced, working in special factories to cast bronze, make pottery, and carve jade and bone exclusively for the royal house. Their occupations were probably passed down from generation to generation. The potter and bronze caster possessed the most advanced technology of their age; they must have been regarded with the same mingling of awe and admiration that we accord the astrophysicist and molecular geneticist today.

THE IMPERIAL WORKSHOPS

During the Han dynasty (206 BC–AD 220), and possibly as early as the Zhou and Shang, craftsmen were organized under a government agency which oversaw the production of objects for the use of the royal house. This network of government workshops stretched throughout the empire, and documents record that every region had a bureau to oversee such work. In addition, under the Han every male adult was required to provide one month's corvée labor per year for government projects, and craftsmen discharged this obligation in the imperial workshops. That these workshops incorporated an elaborate division of labor is evidenced in the many pieces which list participating artisans. In the case of lacquerware, at least seven or eight craftsmen contributed to the production of each piece. The bureaucratic organization of the imperial workshops is seen in the relatively high number of administrators who were recorded as overseeing production – in some cases as many as the number of artisans. The imperial workshops of later centuries, too, were marked by an extensive division of labor. The porcelain vessels produced at the imperial kilns of Jingdezhen in Jiangxi Province, for example, were usually shaped by the hands of scores of artisans. Forming on the wheel, polishing, painting pattern outlines, filling in pattern colors, glazing, and firing comprise only a few of the many production stages.

Gilded bronze kneeling figure, Han dynasty

Opposite: Reconstructing the clay army at the tomb of Qin Shi-huang-di

Scroll detail of bustling city scene at Qing Ming Festival, Song Dynasty

A system of craft patronage by ruler and nobleman had already made its appearance in this early age, and this system was to color the development of Chinese crafts up to modern times. Palace craftsmen continued to work in imperial factories devoted to producing the finest of lacquers, silks, and pottery. Officials were always on the alert for talented artisans, who were recruited for work in the imperial factories. With the certainty of a livelihood and a supply of rare and expensive materials, they could create masterpieces in jade, bronze, lacquer, and cloisonné. Only the most skilled workers could hope to reach this level, after they had mastered their medium through a long and difficult apprenticeship. They were fine artists, and professionals in the best sense of the word.

In the cities private workshops were also established to supply the needs of wealthy merchants, landlords, and officials. The urban craftsman worked with the same costly materials and used the same techniques and motifs as his palace counterpart. With luck, he might receive the patronage of a wealthy merchant; otherwise, he worked in one of the guilds established for protection against the demands of powerful and unscrupulous buyers. These guilds, organized by profession as in the West, thrived particularly after the tenth century and continued to the middle of the twentieth century. The secrets of the craft were transmitted from father to son, or from master to apprentice.

Another type of professional craftsman traveled from location to location, wherever his skills were needed. Whole families – fathers, sons, and grandsons – special-

Above, left: Buddhist grotto art, Yungang. *Above:* Stone carving of Guan-yin, Buddhist Goddess of Mercy, Tang dynasty

ized in certain skills, such as sculpting and making religious images. Such itinerant artisans carved bas-reliefs for tombs throughout China. When Buddhism swept down along the trade routes from Central Asia, it brought the practice of carving Buddhist statues within cave shrines. In the fifth century families of artisans specializing in such Buddhist sculpture were taken as prisoners of war by the Northern Wei rulers and moved first to Yungang, near Datong, Shanxi Province, and later to Longmen, near Luoyang, where they were required to carve monumental stone figures and cave shrines. When Buddhist grotto art was at its peak, every monastery and cave center must have had great numbers of these artisans in residence.

All these craftsmen shared one practice: within the family, skills were passed on only to sons. A skilled artist guarded his trade secrets fiercely, as they were the source of his livelihood. He never revealed his techniques to a daughter, who would marry and leave the family, taking the secrets with her. Women were not permitted to join guilds or work outside the house, though they did embroidery and weaving on a piecework basis for local workshops.

THE GENTLEMAN PAINTER

Traditionally, professional craftsmen were not granted the same high respect as the cultivated amateur painter. Gentlemen painters were not supposed to sell their works of art; they painted only for pleasure and self-expression. The brush alone was exempt from categorization as a mere tool to be used by common artisans. Wielded by the literati in the calligraphy of official documents, in the poetry of personal expression, and in the landscapes of mystical unity with nature, the brush was always the scholar's sword, beyond the reach of the unlettered peasant artist or urban artisan. Because of the literati dominance of the brush, folk painting never developed in China; instead, folk pictures took the form of woodblock prints or scissor cuts.

THE FOLK ARTIST

Painting paper umbrellas

Folk artists traditionally worked on their products during slack periods of the agricultural seasons. Their wares–everyday ceramics, festival lanterns, baskets, and woven goods–were both practical and decorative. Peasant women specialized in embroidery, papercuts, and batik; their skill in these traditional crafts enhanced their marriage possibilities. Men carved woodblocks to print festive New Year pictures and decorated furniture, such as wedding chests, for their fellow villagers. There were always artists among the villagers who could, within the limitations of their simple materials, create new designs or imbue old ones with new life. For the most part, however, designs were transmitted unchanged from father to son and mother to daughter, thus preserving the same motifs, the same stitches, and the same woodblocks. Innovation was not of great importance.

THE HERITAGE OF CHINA'S CRAFTS

Although the forms, purpose, materials, and techniques of China's three artistic traditions were very different, these branches were not entirely isolated. All three groups shared a rich artistic heritage of symbols, motifs, and legends which appeared in all media. Thus the peach, for example, may recur in papercuts, on fine porcelains, or in paintings. In each case, the peach retained the symbolic meaning of longevity. All crafts use the same motifs; carved jade, porcelain, lacquerware, and cloisonné are all related through their shared cultural symbolism.

The principle of *archaism,* or love of the past and its art forms, has always been important in Chinese art. The traditional Chinese view of history idealized the ancient past as a golden age of refinement and culture. Just as the earliest legendary dynasties were considered to be the most culturally and morally refined, so were the earliest art objects the most highly revered. Because of this belief, the re-creation of old objects has always been a highly respectable artistic pursuit. The crafts of the Song and Qing were especially influenced by the archaism of their age, when emperors commissioned thousands of bronzes, porcelains, and jades to be fashioned in the style of earlier pieces. Reproduction is not a mechanical process, however. Rather it is a *creative act*, whereby an object of beauty is given new life in the skilled hands of a later creator.

Making a reproduction of a Tang terra-cotta horse

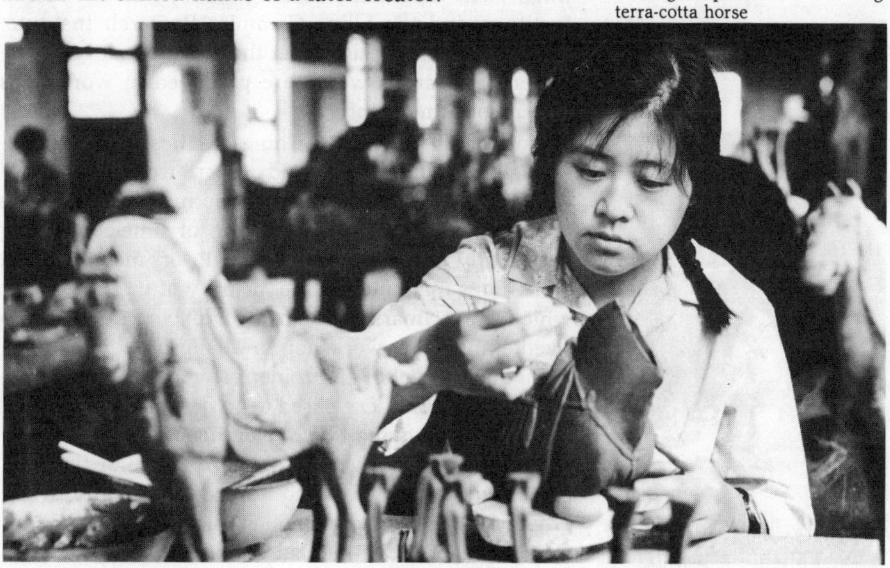

THE CRAFTS TODAY

The arts and crafts discussed in this book are still being made today; some are straightforward re-creations of past masterpieces, and some are new interpretations in traditional styles. Beautiful replicas of the small sculptures of earlier centuries are being produced and sold in craft shops, museums, and foreign outlets all over the world. Artists working in China are breathing new life into statues of Tang horses and court ladies. Reproduction also involves careful scientific research into the details of ancient wares, so that replicas are both beautiful and technically accurate.

Today's young craftworkers study in research institutes throughout China. There is no longer any social division between the artists who work with brushes and those who use cutting tools; both are highly respected. Another profound break with tradition is the participation of women in crafts other than embroidery. Talented young men and women are selected to study in the research institutes under the careful eyes of old master craftsmen. Students learn traditional designs and techniques and then go on to create new patterns and forms. Veteran craftsmen often work with their students to create large pieces for exhibition. Important research institutes include the Shanghai Arts and Crafts Research Institute, the Tianjin Design Institute, the Suzhou Embroidery Research Institute, the Jingdezhen Ceramics Teaching Institute and Research Institute, and the Liling Ceramics Research Institute. Researchers and designers at these centers develop the patterns for crafts which are produced in workshops throughout the country.

A commendation for design master Liu Chuan, displayed at the Shiwan Art Pottery Workshop

Workshops in major Chinese cities like Beijing, Shanghai, Guangzhou, and other traditional craft centers have gathered together the most skilful artists and support them in the creation of time-consuming and costly arts and crafts. Small or medium-sized workshops manufacture the majority of the fine crafts, which are primarily intended for export. A medium-sized embroidery workshop in Changsha, for example, has a department of embroiderers who create extremely fine art embroidery based upon designs often chosen from classic bird-and-flower paintings. The patterns are created by the workshop designers. Some of the final pieces will be one of a kind, for exhibition only, while others will be offered for sale at the trade fairs held for foreign buyers. Commercial considerations greatly influence design at the workshop, just as they did in the porcelain centers of the eighteenth century. The same small workshop also produces embroidery made by special sewing machines, although the work is still very slow. Some mechanization in craftwork is certain to occur as a result of future technological development.

Village crafts still exist as sparetime activities for farm workers, although many have been organized in regional centers to speed production and transportation. Even the old village art of papercutting has moved to regional workshops, where the pictures are prepared in vast quantities for commercial distribution. The woodblock prints so loved by the peasants are also a new industry; in the weeks before the lunar New Year, millions of lithographs are printed for sale in China. The pictures are becoming an increasingly popular export item as well. In the process of increased production, the folk arts are being researched, recorded, refined, shorn of superstitious elements, and imbued with symbols reflecting the new society. In China's research institutes, artists are preserving these hitherto unknown arts and crafts and making them part of the heritage of the whole world.

Women papercutters

FOR FURTHER READING

Dawson, Raymond, ed. *The Legacy of China.* Oxford: Oxford University Press, 1964.

Fitzgerald, C.P. *China: A Short Cultural History.* New York: Praeger, 1961.

Loewe, Michael. *Imperial China: The Historical Background to the Modern Age.* New York: Praeger, 1969.

Meskill, John, ed. *An Introduction to Chinese Civilization.* Lexington, MA: D.C. Heath and Company, 1973.

Needham, Joseph. *Science and Civilization in China,* vol. 4, pt. 2. Cambridge: Cambridge University Press, 1965.

Clay figure, Qin dynasty

CHAPTER 2

CHINA'S ARTISTIC DEVELOPMENT

The history of Chinese arts and crafts shows an amazing continuity of design over tens of centuries. Each generation of artists has added or redefined motifs to reflect the technological innovations of the age. In some eras Western influences can be clearly seen in the design repertoire, while in others Chinese crafts developed independently of the West. The arts and crafts of China today are the unique product of this long history.

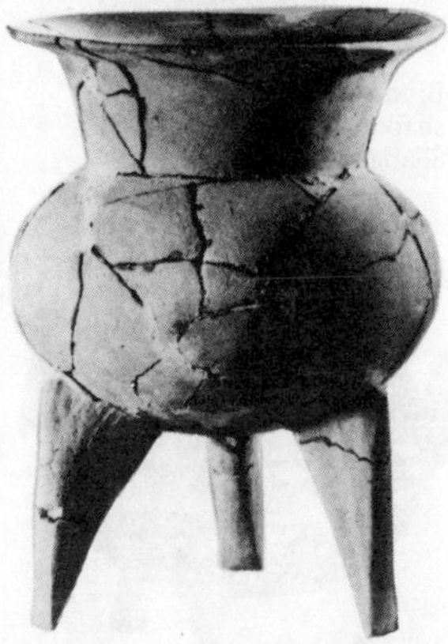

Ceramic *dĭng* tripod, Neolithic era

THE NEOLITHIC PERIOD

During China's Neolithic period, which stretched from the tenth to the second millennium BC, finely executed styles of pottery appeared, foreshadowing the development of ceramics as a major Chinese art form. The ancient pots, incised or painted with geometric and linear designs or stylized animals and fish, show an amazing level of artistic skill. These motifs, together with the shapes such as the *li* and *ding* tripods which first appeared in the Neolithic era, set important stylistic precedents. In this early period jade objects were also being crafted for both ornamental and ritual purposes.

A Neolithic gravesite

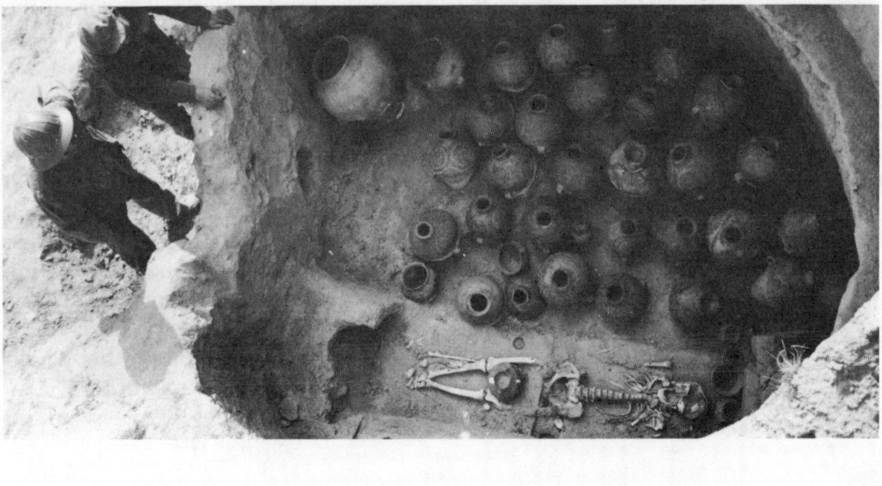

Bronze wine container in the shape of a fantastic animal, Shang dynasty

Bronze *ding* ware with gold inlay, Warring States period

THE ANCIENT DYNASTIES

The appearance of bronze in the second millennium BC during the Shang dynasty marks the end of the Neolithic period in China. A skilled class of Shang craftsmen produced ritual objects of clay, bronze, jade, and wood for the homes and tombs of the nobility. Some examples of Shang pottery approach the technical level of porcelain – thin-bodied, high-fired, and beautifully glazed – while the art of jade carving as seen in ritual objects and ornamental beads and pendants also made great advances. But it is the magnificent bronze ritual vessels of this period that demonstrate a bronze metallurgy so technically advanced that it has never been surpassed. These ritual vessels, thought to possess magical properties, were made to hold sacrificial offerings of food or liquor for the ancestral spirits who consumed only the "essence" of the sacrifice. The Shang king performed these sacrifices to solicit aid from the royal ancestors and spirits of the earth in bringing good fortune in hunting, success in battle, fair weather, and good harvests. These imposing bronzes are most commonly decorated with a *tao-tie* mask – a zoomorphic pattern that meets at a central ridge which represents an animal's nose, flanked by a raised eye on either side. The Shang probably believed that the fearful aspect of the mask helped to ward off evil forces.

In the eleventh century BC, northwestern invaders defeated the Shang and established the Zhou dynasty. Bronze vessels continued to be used in sacrificial rituals, but they were also produced for commemorative purposes. After the seventh century BC, Zhou art was increasingly influenced by the vigorous and more realistic animal designs of the Central Asian nomads.

From the fifth to the third centuries BC, during the Warring States period, the strict rituals of feudal Zhou society were abandoned. As the name implies, this was an age of relentless warfare. It was also a period of tremendous economic growth; agriculture and trade developed, as did the numbers of wealthy merchants who subsidized artisans and commissioned ornamental jade and bronzes. This period of energy and turmoil was one of China's richest eras in the development of arts and crafts. Advances made during the Warring States period laid the basis for excellence in all later crafts. There was a new freedom in design, and regional styles of art appeared. The lacquerware of the period was especially outstanding. Metalworkers also developed sophisticated techniques of openwork in bronze, decorative stone and copper inlay in bronze, and jade inlay in gold. Continued contacts with the nomadic peoples to the north brought lively hunting scenes and animal designs. The wares of the period show a new, fluid grace and realism – a sharp break from the fearsome, stylized, and monumental forms of the Shang and Zhou.

Clay warrior from the tomb of Qin Shi-huang-di

HAN REALISM

Realism reached its first flowering in Chinese art during the Han dynasty (206 BC–AD 220). Under this powerful and cosmopolitan empire, China's borders were pushed westward almost as far as Persia, where realistic design elements originated and were gradually carried back to China. Carved and painted tomb walls from the period depict active scenes of farmers, warriors, and artisans. The tombs of the Han – and of the short-lived Qin dynasty which preceded it – contained vast numbers of ceramic figurines and statues created expressly to accompany and protect the spirits of the dead in the next world. In 1974 an army of realistic, life-size clay archers, foot soldiers, warriors and their mounts was discovered near Xian at the grave site of the founder of the Qin dynasty, Qin Shi-huang-di. This is the largest and most extraordinary discovery of early clay sculpture to date. In Han art dragons, tigers, birds, and snakes were part of a complex system which tied together the seasons, directions, and natural elements. Dragons were of particular importance, as they were thought to possess the power to change shape and size at will and to control the rain. Because of this limitless ability to control natural forces, the dragon's might paralleled the emperor's power on earth; thus the dragon became the official emblem of the emperor and his sons.

The Han dynasty continued the late Zhou appreciation of the aesthetic value of jade, which was carved into delicate and beautiful shapes and used for ornaments. Because of its hardness, weight, and impenetrability, jade had come to symbolize courage, moral steadfastness, and purity. Now jade accouterments of rank such as seals were also valued for their elegance and beauty. This appreciation of form was aided by the invention of the iron drill, which allowed the craftsman greater freedom for technical virtuosity and imagination in his work. The art of silk production, which had developed in China in the shadows of prehistory, flour-

Bronze dancers, Han dynasty

ished in the Han dynasty. Bolts of gossamer-thin silk, patterned brocades, and silken embroidery were carried west across Asia along the fabled "Silk Road" to clothe the patrician matrons of Rome.

Aften the fall of the Han, the new mandarin class of well educated, literary, and artistic gentlemen lost interest in the strict morality and rigid social hierarchy of Confucianism. Daoism (Taoism), a philosophy based on mysticism and harmony with nature, and Buddhism, transmitted from India by the first century AD, played an important role in the development of a new Chinese aesthetic. In the course of the three and a half centuries of political instability that followed the end of the Han dynasty, Chinese landscape painting, with its emphasis on the beauties of nature, was established as a vital and important art form.

THE TANG GOLDEN AGE

The Tang dynasty (618–907) was a period of great stability, prosperity, and strength, a time later known as China's Golden Age. The cosmopolitan Tang court sampled the wonders of India, Arabia, Persia, and Southeast Asia. Chinese artisans fashioned bronze and gold mirrors, jewelry, ornaments, and vessels, often using motifs and metalworking techniques adopted from the Near East. The vigorous Tang style is preserved in lively tomb figures decorated with

Multicolor pottery figures, Tang dynasty

multicolored glazes. Subjects include camels and horses, Central Asian and Indian merchants, musicians, dancers, and mounted polo players. Even the ceramic vessels of the Tang reveal confidence and vitality in their expansive shapes and bold colors. Buddhism continued to be a major influence, particularly in painting and the monumental sculptures which still exist in caves and temples all over China.

SONG ELEGANCE

In contrast to the expansive confidence of the Tang, exclusivity and deep nationalism prevailed in the Song dynasty (960–1279). This is the great age of Chinese landscape painting and the classic period of ceramics. The Imperial Academy dictated form and subject; Emperor Hui-zong himself set the tone of purity, elegance, and restraint which was the hallmark of academy painting. Artists of the imperial court carefully followed the example of past masters, depicting bird-and-flower scenes in meticulous detail. By contrast, artists of the Northern Song painted landscapes that were immense, realistic, and pulsing with intensity – overwhelming mountains and jagged precipices. The landscape paintings of the Southern Song convey a softer, more intimate mood, one that is tinged with melancholy. Mountains are girded in mist as sky and water fuse into a single atmospheric continuum. Finally,

Water pot of white *ding* porcelain, Song dynasty

"The North Sea," by Zhou Chen, Ming dynasty

the Song school of painters influenced by Chan (Zen) Buddhism created works of brilliant insight and spontaneity.

In ceramics this was a period of consolidation of earlier techniques and refinement of form and color. Potters had perfected the construction of stoneware bodies in previous centuries, while green and multicolored glazes were refined during the Tang. Also during the Tang came the discovery of true porcelain—translucent, resonant, and thin bodied. It was left to the Song potter, however, to create the fine porcelain vessels whose classical elegance and exquisite glazes are so highly prized today. Literally thousands of kiln sites were spread throughout northern and southern China. Fine porcelains of bluish-white hue and crackled gray-blue were produced, as well as aqua wares splashed with vivid purple or scarlet. Perhaps the most famous of Song ceramics are the green-glazed wares known as celadons produced in imperial factories or workshops by master artisans, as were the finest bronzes, jade and ivory carvings, lacquerware, silks, and embroidery.

THE YUAN DYNASTY

In 1279 the Song dynasty fell before Mongol invaders from the north. Under the century-long Yuan dynasty which the Mongols established, artistic styles were dominated by lavish decoration. Ceramicists expanded upon the Song technique of painting designs in red or blue under a final glaze, and these wares, especially the blue-and-white porcelains, were highly prized throughout the world.

MING THROUGH QING

Ewer of blue-and-white porcelain, Ming dynasty

The Ming reestablished Han Chinese rule in the fourteenth century. During the Ming dynasty special kilns were established at Jingdezhen in Jiangxi Province for the production of imperial wares, and soon the town surpassed all other pottery centers in both quantity and quality. Fluid, white porcelain vessels and figurines were produced in Fujian Province and exported throughout the world. Cloisonné and enamelware, introduced from the West during the Yuan dynasty, reveal the Ming taste for richly colored floral motifs and the popular cobalt blue so common in porcelain of this period. The perfection of weaving techniques is evident in the vividly embroidered silk robes worn by Ming emperors and nobles. A type of silk tapestry known as *ke-si* or "cut silk" was sometimes used to form the emblems of rank or "mandarin squares" which adorned official robes.

THE FINAL FLOWERING

Jade vessel in ancient style, Qing dynasty

The Qing dynasty, established by the Manchus in the seventeenth century, was the last of China's dynasties. During the seventeenth and eighteenth centuries the court initiated a spirit of conservatism – a final flowering of the decorative arts. The Yuan practice of conscripting craftsmen continued in the Ming and Qing dynasties. The Kang-xi emperor, who ruled from 1662 to 1722, established an extensive complex of imperial workshops at the palace; objects of bronze, glass, gold, enamel, lacquer, jade, and ivory were produced for the use of the court. The Qian-long emperor, who ruled from 1736 to 1795, was especially zealous in his patronage of luxurious crafts, and the resultant output

was prodigious. Qian-long greatly admired the strange and the new, and imperial workshops were ingenious in complying with his tastes. Their goods were unsurpassed in virtuosity. Porcelains and lacquerware were produced both for the court and for the tremendous export market of this period. Cloisonné also evidenced the polished smoothness characteristic of early Qing art. Elaborately embroidered court robes, already well developed in the Ming, featured colorful dragons, tigers, cranes, and other animals as symbols of official rank.

The nineteenth century brought gradual stagnation in the crafts, as sheer technique replaced creative force. The many luxury items produced for export show the growing influence of European designs. Elaborate decoration and intricate shapes, although masterful, could not conceal the artistic decline already in evidence by the end of Qian-long's reign.

FOLK ART

Throughout China's art history runs a vigorous parallel tradition of folk arts and crafts made of inexpensive local materials. Folks artists usually worked on such projects during the winter and in their spare time, fashioning dough, wood, clay, and common stone for their own use or for sale in local markets. Unlike the imperial and urban craftsmen, who generally represented a more uniform and homogeneous artistic tradition, folk artists were markedly regional in their materials, subjects, and techniques, and their art was enriched by the folk art of non-Han minority peoples throughout China. A robust folk stoneware decorated with bold floral patterns was produced in many areas of northern China. True rag paper was invented in AD 105 and further refined in the Tang dynasty. By the time of the Song, this excellent and relatively inexpensive material was commonly used by folk artists. Papercuts, lanterns, kites, and woodblock prints were often designed for use at traditional festivals, such as the Springtime Qing Ming (Purity and Brightness) Festival, the summer Dragon Boat Festival, the Mid-Autumn Festival, and the important Chinese New Year celebration. Such crafts have been a continuing source of vitality and imagination throughout China's history.

Contemporary indigo print with double-fish design

Woodcut from time of Sino-Japanese war

TWENTIETH CENTURY ART

With the twentieth century came foreign influences, and later a spirit of innovation. The Shanghai School of painting, which had taken shape in the second part of

Contemporary papercut

the nineteenth century, encouraged artists to employ traditional techniques to express their inner feelings. Among China's most famous modern painters was Qi Baishi, born in 1863 into a peasant family in Hunan Province. His unconventional paintings of birds, flowers, shrimp, and insects pared down to their barest essentials capture the vitality of these humble creatures. Except for a few creative forces like Qi Baishi, however, Chinese painters in the early years of this century were caught up in turmoil and social upheaval, and art work seemed unimportant in comparison. In the years following World War I, the level of social ferment increased in China. In the 1920s a new movement for social change emerged in the cities, and the woodcut movement was part of this new drive. Influenced by a powerful European style, the new woodcuts presented a sharp contrast to all preceding Chinese art. Inexpensive and easy to produce, woodcuts answered a practical need. They were the perfect vehicle for social criticism in this turbulent period – a folk art form with a political message. When the Communists established an art academy at Yanan in the 1930s, woodcut artists began to adapt and incorporate folk elements into their designs.

In the years since 1949 great woodcut artists have emerged, while the style of traditional landscapes has

Huxian peasant painters

also been maintained. Landscapes now incorporate modern elements of the new society: red flags, modern tractors, and vast bridges appear among mountains clothed in mist. Famous painters have preserved the tradition of the Shanghai School, and animals are a popular subject, from yaks to donkeys, camels, owls, and goldfish. Peasant painters have also been actively experimenting with folk forms derived from papercuts and New Year woodblock pictures. The peasant paintings of Huxian near Xian reveal bustling, colorful rural scenes, which have won international acclaim. No new national style in the fine arts has appeared as yet, however, and no one style has become dominant over the others. China's artists are still seeking a formula for combining the old and the new – the outcome of the experiment remains to be seen.

CRAFTS IN THE NEW CHINA

By the early twentieth century, most of China's guilds and workshops were merely producing pieces for export using foreign designs and colors or mechanically turning out quantities of mediocre, uninspired products for domestic use. Skilled craftsmen needed the patronage of the court or wealthy merchants to survive, because their techniques were time-consuming and their materials costly. Without this support craftsmen were reduced to making items such as jewelry, chopsticks, and mahjong pieces just to stay alive. Quality declined and patterns dwindled to a few standardized themes such as fat Buddhas and languid goddesses. A century of foreign domination followed by a decade of Japanese occupation had smothered the last embers of vitality in the ancient Chinese decorative arts.

Such was the situation when the People's Republic of China set about to revive the arts and crafts industry in 1950. First, research institutes were established in old craft centers throughout the country to preserve traditional arts while modernizing techniques. Master artisans were gathered together, and once they were assured of a guaranteed income, they began to transmit the ancient skills and secret techniques to a new generation of Chinese youth. Feudal or superstitious elements were removed from the old designs, and fresh symbols were drawn from legends and folk traditions to promote socialist goals. Small workshops were linked together into cooperative units. In Beijing numerous old cloisonné and jade carving workshops were organized to form the Beijing Handicraft Company. This company worked with local craftsmen to overcome artistic stagnation and recapture the vigor and authentic styles of early crafts. In the spring of 1951 an exhibition of wall paintings from the old Buddhist caves at Dunhuang in northwest China came to Beijing. These designs provided an exciting stimulus to local craftsmen, who immediately began to use these ancient and colorful designs on cloisonné vases, lacquer trays, lamps, and tea containers.

In 1953 arts and crafts from all over China were gathered for exhibition in Beijing. On display were objects made by artisans from twenty-four national minorities, in twenty-eight provinces and autonomous regions. Porcelains from Jingdezhen, Yixing teapots, and Shiwan figurines were on display, all products of newly revitalized kilns. Bamboo and straw work from Sichuan, lacquerware from Yangzhou and Fuzhou, boxwood and soapstone carvings from Zhejiang, and embroidery from many areas were just a few of the more than three thousand objects in the exhibition. Craft workers came to Beijing to see art from other parts of China, exchange ideas, and view the ancient art in the Palace Museum that they had never seen before. Emphasis was placed on revitalizing design. Embroidery workers studied robes that had been made in the Qing imperial workshops; potters studied glazes previously used only in imperial kilns.

THE PAST SERVES THE PRESENT

Old production centers which had long lain dormant have now been revived with government support. The famous kilns of the Song dynasty celadon center of Longquan in Zhejiang Province, for example, which had been idle for some three hundred years, were back in production in 1959. In addition, a network of arts and crafts research institutes has been established, so that artisans, designers, and students can determine the exact nature of old wares. Only when authentic ancient forms have been clearly established do the researchers begin to re-create their shapes and decor in modern pieces. The institutes also experiment with new items, determining patterns, materials, and subjects. Then a prototype is created under factory conditions and, if successful, is adopted for large-scale production. Some of China's most beautiful and exciting art pieces are being produced in these institutes.

Blue porcelain dragon plate, Hunan Province

Recent government directives have called for the revival of small, locally run concerns known as collective enterprises, of which craft workshops are an important component. Such enterprises are being promoted both in the cities and on the communes, where they will become increasingly important as agriculture becomes more mechanized. Today's generation is combining ancient craft traditions with advanced scientific techniques. If these new artisans maintain the spirit of artistic integrity and innovation that has long characterized China's craft industry, this new synthesis will be exciting to see.

FOR FURTHER READING

Lee, Sherman. *A History of Far Eastern Art.* Englewood Cliffs, NJ: Prentice Hall, 1973.

New Archeological Finds in China, Part II. Beijing: Foreign Languages Press, 1978.

Selection of Archeological Finds of the People's Republic of China. Beijing: Wen Wu Press, 1976.

Sickman, Laurence and Soper, Alexander. *The Art and Architecture of China.* New York: Penguin Books, 1971.

Sullivan, Michael. *The Arts of China.* Revised edition. Berkeley, CA: University of California Press, 1977.

壽
一團和氣

CHAPTER 3

MOTIFS AND SYMBOLS IN CHINESE ART

The decorations and motifs used in Chinese crafts carry messages whose meanings are quickly apparent to anyone familiar with Chinese culture. Many decorative elements are symbols that originate in some aspect of Chinese folklore or history. Some are actually complex word plays. The rich heritage and variety of artistic symbols are a special feature of Chinese arts and crafts.

Neolithic pot

Designs quickly became stylized. For example, simple fish and animal shapes painted on Neolithic pottery were often reduced to a few geometric lines repeated to form a pattern. The first Chinese characters, carved over four thousand years ago on ox bones and tortoise shells, were signs which had come to represent an object or an idea. Areas of early Chinese civilization along the Yellow River were subject to flood and drought; hence it is not surprising that the Chinese people, whose survival depended on agriculture, were very concerned with nature, particularly rain, thunder, and clouds. Many early design elements are really stylized ways to depict nature. The *lei-wen* or thunder pattern, first seen in Neolithic times, is still in use today. The meanings of many of these geometric patterns are still known, though many have been lost in time.

Pottery and textiles, the first sophisticated crafts, formalized the rich artistic vocabulary which was later used in all crafts. A wealth of new designs and symbols was added by the craftsmen of the cosmopolitan Han dynasty, who felt the influence of Central Asia, and by the Buddhists, who brought religious and artistic motifs from India. These new forms were transformed by the Chinese view of nature and aesthetics. The complex Chinese religious beliefs and theories about the forces of nature were woven together and represented in symbolic form over two thousand years ago. Table 1 shows how colors, directions, seasons, and even living creatures were related to the five elements of nature.

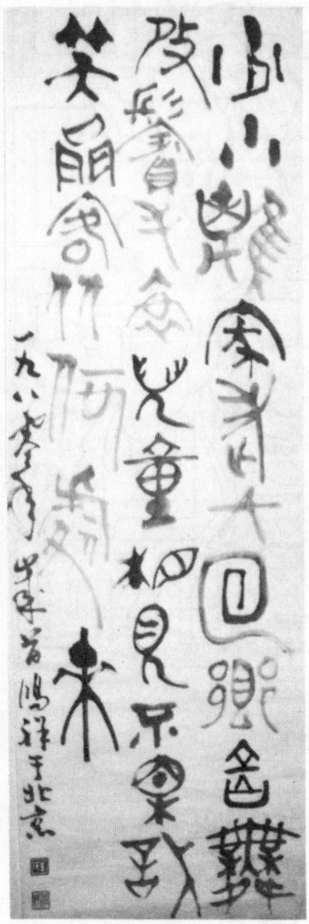

Modern calligraphy in ancient, pictographic style by Zhu Hongxiang

The motifs and symbols of China are seen everywhere, repeated in all crafts and arts shared by

TABLE 1
Five Elements of Nature

wood	*fire*	*earth*	*metal*	*water*
spring	summer	– – –	autumn	winter
east	south	center	west	north
green	red	yellow	white	black
Green Dragon	Red Bird	Yellow Dragon	White Tiger	Black Tortoise

Peonies from collar of Chinese Opera robe

both emperor and villager. The sinuous, coiling dragon, for example, appears embroidered on imperial robes as the emperor's personal emblem, cast in bronze, painted on porcelain vessels, carved on jade and lacquer, and worked in cloisonné. Pattern books used by artisans for embroidery, wood carving, and papercuts formalized the use of certain symbols in each craft.

Symbols like the dragon appear in the earliest Chinese arts and crafts and continue on down through the ages, only slightly altered in form. Of course, there was always room for creative minds to bring about limited innovation and refinement within the boundaries of the traditional representation. In fact, wares can sometimes be dated according to the type and form of motifs used. The awesome, menacing dragon of early bronze vessels later became a mysterious rain-bearing creature darting in and out of the clouds, and later still, the proud emblem of imperial majesty.

There are several kinds of symbols used throughout Chinese arts and crafts. One type uses a rebus–a homophone which expresses a secret message or double meaning. For example, the red bats often seen on late Ming and Qing ceramics play on similarities in sound: "red bat" (*hong-fu* 紅蝠) sounds the same as "abundant good fortune" (*hong-fu* 洪福). This, in fact, is the symbolic meaning of what appears to be merely a simple decorative element. Another example is the goldfish (*jin-yu* 金魚) which in Chinese sounds like "gold in abundance" (*jin-yu* 金余), and thus the goldfish really symbolizes a wish for prosperity.

China's rich literary and historical heritage also provides a wealth of stories and symbols used in art. Famous generals, sages, and poets have acquired a godlike position through the centuries and appear as motifs on many types of crafts. Folktales also provide the background for such charming figures as the Weaving Maid and the Herd Boy. The two are only allowed

Herd Boy and Weaving Maid meet on the border of the Milky Way

to meet once a year, on the seventh day of the seventh month, when flocks of magpies form a floating bridge in heaven so that the Weaving Maid can cross over the Milky Way to see her beloved Herd Boy. Because of their assistance to the unfortunate lovers, magpies are known as symbols of marital happiness, and pairs of birds carrying ribbons or cords are used to represent marriage ties.

The special flavor of Chinese craft design comes from its symbolism. Seldom are patterns used purely for decoration; there is almost always some underlying theme or message, if one looks hard to discover it. Some of the major symbols are discussed here.

TREES AND FLOWERS

All flowers are used as motifs in crafts from embroidery to porcelain. Of special importance are the Flowers of the Four Seasons: plum blossom or prunus, symbol of winter; peony, symbol of spring; lotus, which represents summer; and chrysanthemum, symbolizing autumn. Flowers are associated with beautiful women.

PLUM BLOSSOM

In the depths of winter, the prunus, or plum blossom, puts forth new flowers from seemingly dead branches. The beautiful five-petaled blossoms, scattered on twisted, knotted branches, represent new life at the end of winter. A popular blue-and-white porcelain design of prunus against a network of lines (crackle) shows new blossoms against the breaking ice of early spring. Hence the plum blossom symbolizes winter and beauty.

The enduring beauty of the plum is seen in the following description from an old painting manual:

> When the plum tree is painted on a cliff or at the edge of water, its branches are curiously twisted and bear few blossoms. . . . When the plum tree is painted "combed by the wind" or "washed by the rain," there are many spaces on the branches, blossoms are wide open, and some of them crushed. When the plum tree is painted in mist, branches are delicately drawn and the blossoms depicted with tenderness as though they held smiles and gentle laughter on the boughs.[1]

[1] Mai-mai Sze, trans. and ed., *The Mustard Seed Garden Manual of Painting* (Princeton: Princeton University Press, 1963), p. 401.

PINE TREE

Because it retains its green foliage year round, the pine tree represents endurance and longevity. Especially loved are the ancient and gnarled pines which seem perilously perched on steep mountain cliffs. Although buffeted by winds and storm, they thrive year after year, nourished by pure mountain air and clear springs. Thus the pine also represents pure life and constancy in the face of adversity.

BAMBOO

The bamboo, with its slender stems and lush covering of delicate leaves, represents vigor and durability. Dense groves of bamboo are found throughout central and southern China, often reaching a height of more than one hundred feet. These fine plants symbolize resilience and integrity because they bend in the wind but return to an upright position.

Because of the delicacy and complexity of the bamboo's shape, only a fine artist could capture its likeness. Even more than technique, the artist had to possess a calm mind focused on the subject so that the strokes were completed in the span of breath. Students were instructed this way in an old painting manual:

> Avoid making stems like drumsticks. Avoid making joints of equal length. Avoid lining up the bamboos like a fence. Avoid placing the leaves all to one side. Avoid making them like *hsing,* or like dragonfly wings, or like the fingers of an outstretched hand, or like the crisscrossing of a net. . . . At the moment of putting brush to paper or silk, do not hesitate.[2]

[2]Mai-mai Sze, *The Mustard Seed Garden Manual,* p. 369.

THREE FRIENDS OF WINTER

The prunus, pine, and bamboo are known as the "three friends of winter." Together they represent happiness and endurance in old age, because all three live and bloom in winter – or old age. A porcelain vase with the "three friends" motif was often given as a token of friendship.

POMEGRANATE

Because the pomegranate has many seeds, it is associated with fertility and prosperity. The Chinese character for "seed" also means "sons," hence the fruit symbolizes the wish for many sons. Pillowcases embroidered with pomegranates are given as wedding gifts.

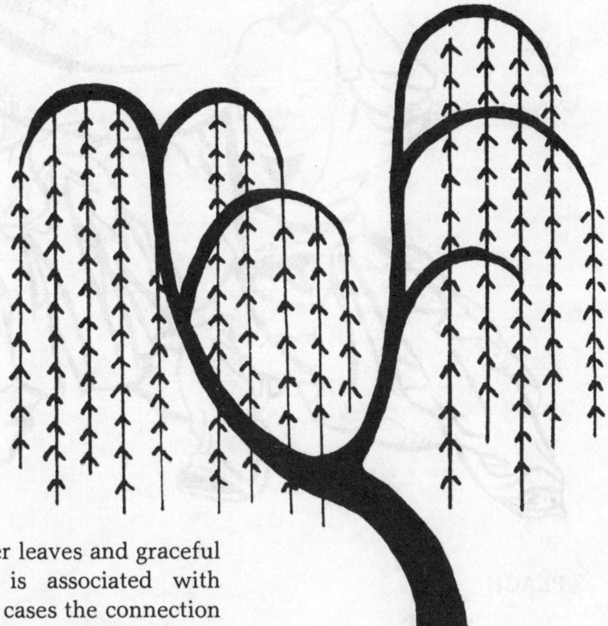

WILLOW TREE

Because of its long, slender leaves and graceful sway, the willow tree is associated with feminine beauty. In some cases the connection is further limited to the "singsong" girls or cultivated courtesans who lived in the "willow quarters." The willow was also a symbol of friendship, and willow boughs were presented to a traveler upon his departure.

Thought to have cleansing powers, the willow was used to brush off the ancestral tombs at the Qing Ming Festival in springtime. The wood of the willow was believed to enable shamans to communicate with the spirit world.

The willow tree was frequently seen in landscape painting and on porcelain. The blue-and-white willowware porcelains produced in England in the late eighteenth century had a design based upon a story of young lovers facing many obstacles to their marriage. The willow pattern became almost synonymous with Chinese porcelain in the mind of the average Westerner.

PEACH

Luscious and vibrantly red, the peach is one of the most important Chinese symbols. Old legends describe a magic peach tree which grows in the paradise of Xi Wang Mu, the Royal Mother of the West. This tree, said to bloom only once every three thousand years and to bear fruit only after another three thousand years, yields the peaches of immortality. The God of Longevity, Shou Lao, is often depicted carrying a huge peach or even emerging from a peach. Thus the peach symbol represents a wish for a long and healthy life. This symbol, which is used in all Chinese crafts, is also associated with marriage. One of the most interesting forms occurs in a graceful Yixing stoneware teapot molded to resemble a whole peach. Amulets and beads of peach pits were carved by village craftsmen to protect children from evil spirits. Today intricately carved peach pit necklaces are popular jewelry items for export.

LOTUS

Because it rises out of the mud to bloom undefiled, the lotus symbolizes purity amid the corruption of worldly life. The flower draws much of its importance from Buddhism; the lotus is the sacred emblem of Buddhism and the sign of perfection. The Buddha's throne is also pictured as a large, flattened lotus with petals emanating on all sides.

The lotus has several other meanings, which are derived by use of a play upon the Chinese words for lotus: *lian* or *he*. The phrase *lian sheng gui zi* refers to the lotus, mouth organ, and cassia, often arranged in the motif of a child carrying these objects. Through a play on words the same phrase means, "For successive generations may you give birth to sons who attain high rank." The motif, often used in late Ming and Qing crafts, represents a wish for fertility and prosperity. Another rebus is based upon the phrase *he-ping* or "lotus vase," which is pronounced like the word for peace. Thus a lotus vase may convey the wish for peace and tranquility.

The lotus is associated also with the summer season. The lotus petal shape is seen in panels on ceramics, and the lotus motif itself is used in almost every craft.

CHRYSANTHEMUM

To the Chinese the lovely chrysanthemum signifies longevity and a life spent in quiet retirement. The flower is associated with autumn, and the ninth lunar month is called the chrysanthemum month. This is the time for strollers to appreciate the colorful blooms of gold, white, pink, pale green, purple, or white with red streaks. Because it defies the frost to bloom triumphantly in autumn, the chrysanthemum is the floral symbol of the autumn season.

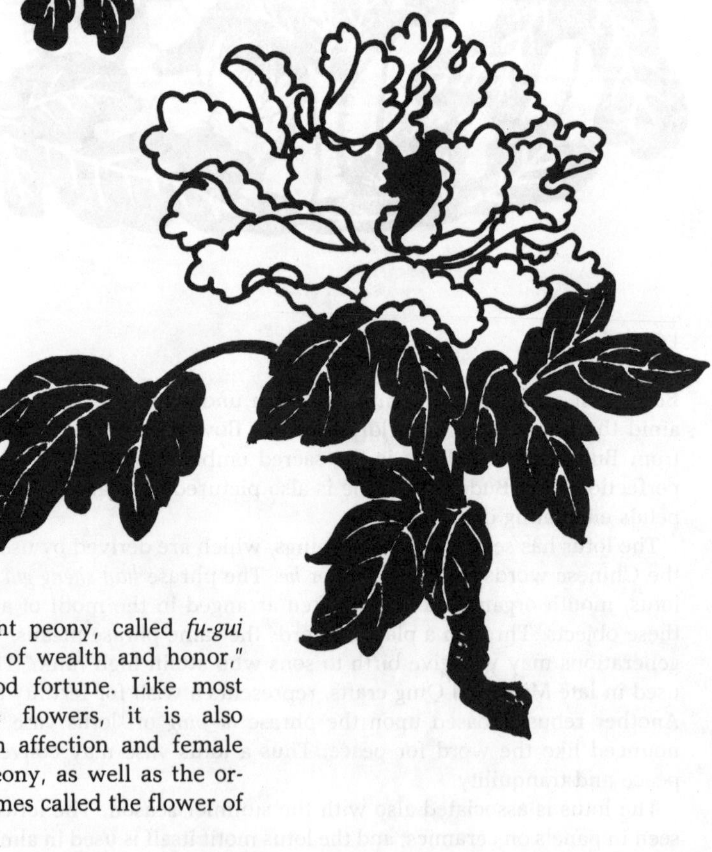

PEONY

The magnificent peony, called *fu-gui hua* or "flower of wealth and honor," symbolizes good fortune. Like most other Chinese flowers, it is also associated with affection and female beauty. The peony, as well as the orchid, is sometimes called the flower of spring.

ORCHID

The long, fluid leaves and softly curling petals of the orchid plant are popular themes in Chinese art. This fragrant flower has for centuries represented the virtue, moral excellence, and refinement of the superior man, whose reputation precedes him like perfume. Sometimes used as a symbol of spring, the orchid is also associated with a woman's beauty:

> Leaves are painted in a few strokes, and they should have a floating grace in rhythm with the wind, (moving like a goddess) in rainbow-hued skirt with a moon-shaped jade ornament swinging from her belt. No breath of ordinary air touches them. . . . Dotting the heart of the orchid is like drawing in the eyes of a beautiful woman. . . . The whole essence of the flower is contained in that small touch.[3]

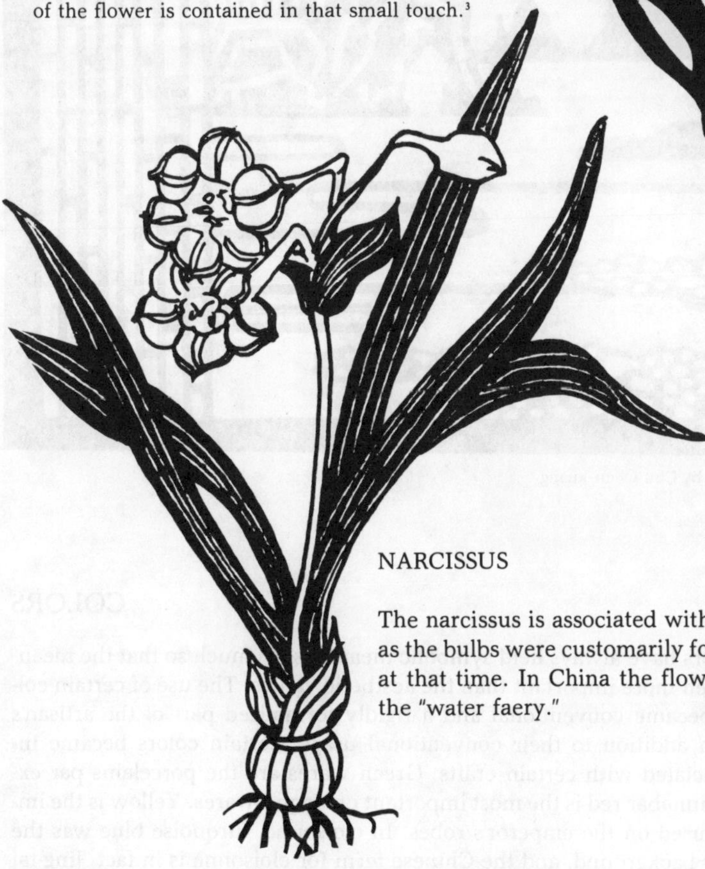

NARCISSUS

The narcissus is associated with the New Year, as the bulbs were customarily forced into bloom at that time. In China the flower also is called the "water faery."

[3]Mai-mai Sze, *The Mustard Seed Garden Manual,* pp. 325-26.

Guilin landscape by Chu Chen-kuang

COLORS

In China colors have always held symbolic meanings, so much so that the meanings were often more important than the aesthetic values. The use of certain colors quickly became conventional and a rigidly formalized part of the artisan's repertoire. In addition to their conventional usage, certain colors became intimately associated with certain crafts. Green wares are the porcelains par excellence, as cinnabar red is the most important of lacquerwares. Yellow is the imperial color, used on the emperor's robes. In cloisonné, turquoise blue was the most popular background, and the Chinese term for cloisonné is in fact "Jing-tai blue," which means turquoise blue.

GREEN

Green is the color of nature in the growing phase, of spring and the east. The Chinese word *qing* actually covers a whole spectrum from blue, green, gray, or neutral colors to black. This is a broad category describing natural scenery, often seen at a distance, and in many instances indicates blue tones, especially azure.

The word *qing* also indicates youth and activity. Green and jade have been intimately connected since the earliest times in China. Alchemists in China's middle ages tried to duplicate jade in green pottery and blended their secret potions in green vessels thought to possess the magic properties of jade.

RED

Red is the color of nature in its greatest period of growth, of blazing summer, and of the south. It is the color of celebration and happiness. Red has traditionally been associated with flowers and festivals, and with beautiful women. Bright red cinnabar, or *dan,* was equated with the elixir of immortality; it was the most important ingredient in the alchemists' magic potions.

YELLOW

Yellow is the color of the loess soil of the north China plain, which is the cultural and spiritual home of the Han Chinese. Because it is bound up with the continuing reverence for the soil, the earth itself, yellow has always been very important in Chinese art. Yellow is also associated with the emperor; to make a yellow robe for a commoner would have been unthinkable.

WHITE

White is the color of the spiritual realm, of death and funerals, of autumn and the west. From Buddhism came the idea of purity, by association with the lotus. White is also connected with the finest jades, which were pale white or cream-colored.

BLACK

Black is the color of deep mystery, of winter and the north. It is the color of nature in deepest dormancy, portending spring's vigor. Black thus embodies the potentiality of all things and is the basis of all activity or growth.

Animals appear very early in symbolic form as emblems of status and as astronomical signs. They are frequently used in jade sculpture and on official robes. Animal motifs are greatly favored by the folk artist, who uses them as designs on lanterns, embroidery, and papercuts.

DRAGON

The dragon is undoubtedly the most frequent and important of all Chinese artistic symbols. Unlike the dragon of Western medieval tales, the Chinese dragon is a creature of good who has the power of transformation and brings life-giving rains. Often depicted in pairs, coiling amid clouds or sporting among waves, the dragons compete for a disc which was originally a sun symbol. This design probably represented the struggle between clouds and sun during a storm. Later, however, the flaming disc was identified as a pearl of wisdom or power. Sometimes pictured half hidden in the clouds, the dragon seems caught at the moment of its transfiguration. At such a moment the dragon is more than capable of change – it is change itself.

> . . . the cloud dragon, floating in watery vapours, like a dense mist;
> Billowing formlessly, with thunder-roll and lightning-flash, high aloft he races;
> Mounting the void, treading the dark sky, spurning the turbid vapours, swimming in the clear ones, he enters the House of God;
> Shaking his wings and beating with his pinions, racing the wind, driving the rain, he wanders without end.[4]

Because of its connection with the creative forces of nature, the dragon, in particular a green dragon, was the symbol of the east and spring.

Ancient dragons depicted on bronzes and jade had several forms. Some were one-legged with horns, while others were long, hornless, reptilian creatures, more like serpents. During the Han dynasty the dragon became associated with the emperor's power, and the symbol was adopted to represent the emperor and his sons. Over the centuries a rigid protocol developed; by the time of the Ming and Qing, the dragon – especially the five-clawed variety – had become exclusively the imperial symbol. There were thought to be nine different varieties of dragons, and the emperor alone was permitted to use all nine in decoration. The nine-dragon decoration is seen today on the spectacular screen of glazed tiles in Beijing's Forbidden City. The magnificent coiling dragon is found throughout Chinese crafts, in every medium, with a dominance befitting its position as the emblem of the Son of Heaven and of China itself.

[4]David Hawkes, *Ch'u Tz'u: The Songs of The South* (Boston: Beacon Press, 1962), p. 169.

PHOENIX

As the symbol of the empress, the phoenix appears paired with the majestic imperial dragon. The creature is also said to appear only in times of peace, like the unicorn, and thus symbolizes order and harmony in the world. The bird is actually a composite design, including features of both the pheasant and the peacock. It is a popular motif in embroidery, textiles, and ceramics.

TWELVE ANIMALS OF THE ZODIAC

The Chinese zodiac is a twelve-year cycle in which each year is associated with a specific animal. Those born during the year of a certain animal were thought to share some of the qualities of that animal. The twelve animals are the rat, ox, tiger, hare, dragon, serpent, horse, goat, monkey, cock, dog, and pig.

UNICORN

The gentle unicorn, or *qilin,* is a rare creature, symbol of order and harmony brought about by a virtuous ruler. The creature is a composite design, with the body of a deer, the head of a dragon, and the legs and hooves of a horse. According to legend, the unicorn was often seen during the time of the sage kings Yao and Shun, and appeared again at the birth of Confucius. As society became increasingly dissolute, the creature was seldom seen in later years.

Because the unicorn was thought to live for a thousand years, it also symbolizes longevity. The unicorn is a frequent decoration on ceramics and embroidery.

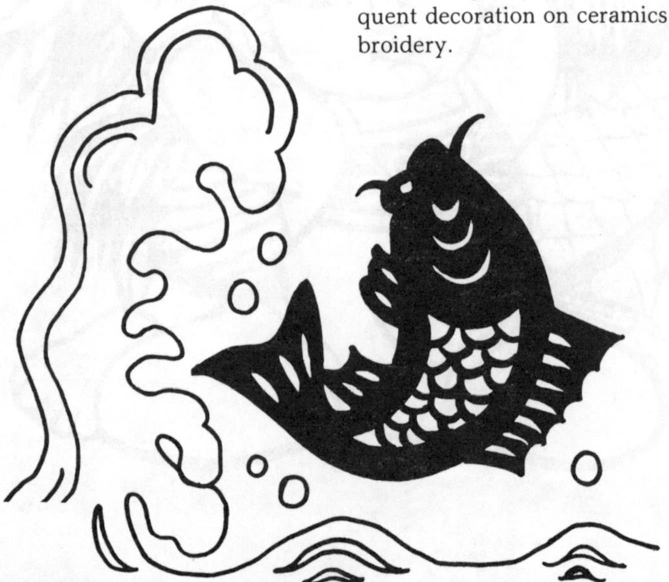

CARP

The Chinese carp has several symbolic values. According to legend, messages were placed in the bellies of the fish, and thus the fish has come to symbolize communication with a distant friend or loved one. Because of the fish's scales and whiskers, it is thought to resemble a dragon and symbolizes strength and perseverance. The carp that braves the current of the Yellow River to leap up the falls at Longmen (the Dragon Gate) was thought to be transformed into a kind of fish-dragon. Thus the design of carp passing over the Dragon Gate symbolized success at examinations and achievement of a civil appointment. When this decoration was added to a gift for a scholar, it represented a wish for success in literary and official endeavor.

CRANE

The graceful white crane is the symbol of immortality. The bird is often pictured carrying sages off to the Three Islands of the Immortals in the Eastern Ocean. Frequently the crane is grouped with the pine tree, the spotted deer, the tortoise, and the *ling-zhi* fungus, all symbols of immortality.

FU DOG

The so-called Fu dog or Fu lion was originally a Buddhist symbol. The name, Fu, actually means Buddha; once the guardian of Buddhist temples, the creature came to symbolize courage and strength and was used to guard gates of temples, sacred areas, and official residences throughout China. The ferocious temple guardian of bronze or stone is rendered more tamely elsewhere as a playful dog resembling the Pekingese. When pictured this way, the male often sports with a brocade ball, while the female is paired with her cub.

BAT

Owing to a play on words, the bat is a symbol of good fortune. In Chinese, the phrase "red bat" (*hong-fu* 红 蝠) is pronounced like "abundant good fortune" (*hong-fu* 洪福). This auspicious decoration is frequently seen on porcelains of the Qing. A decoration with five bats also stems from a play on words: the five bats (*wu-fu* 五蝠) represent the five forms of good fortune (*wu-fu* 五福)—tranquility, wealth, longevity, love of virtue, and a natural death. The bat is seen on ceramics, textiles, wood, and lacquer.

HORSE

The horse is a symbol of persistence, swiftness, and intelligence. Of special importance are the eight famous horses which carried the legendary King Mu to visit Xi Wang Mu, the Royal Mother of the West. These steeds are often seen on ceramics. The horse was also a popular subject in early jade carving.

BUTTERFLY

The butterfly is a symbol of longevity, perhaps owing to a play on words between butterfly (*hu-die* 蝴蝶) and octogenarian (*die* 耋). The butterfly is also associated with summer and happiness. The Daoist philosopher Zhuang-zi recalled a wonderful dream in which he was a butterfly happily soaring from place to place, with no knowledge of who he was. Suddenly he woke up and knew he was Zhuang-zi. Was it Zhuang-zi who dreamed he was a butterfly, or was it the butterfly who dreamed he was Zhuang-zi? The philosopher used this story to demonstrate the uncertainty of knowledge and the happiness of ignorance. The butterfly is a favorite design in papercuts and folk embroidery patterns.

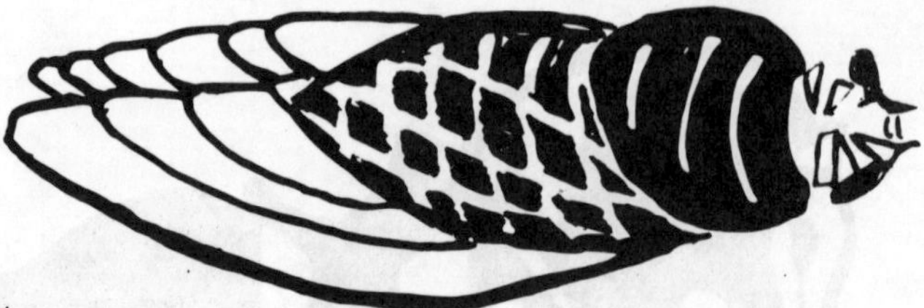

CICADA

Owing to the insect's ability to shed its skin at maturity, the cicada is an ancient symbol of regeneration. Graceful cicadas carved of jade were thought to prevent the degeneration of a corpse or perhaps to speed its rebirth in another world. The cicada, also admired for its rhythmic music, is a symbol of happiness and immortality.

HARE

A symbol of intelligence and longevity, the hare is also associated with the moon, where a jade hare is said to pound the drug of immortality beneath a cassia tree. The hare is seen on porcelain and jade, often within a circle representing the moon.

MANDARIN DUCKS

Almost always paired as male and female, mandarin ducks represent marital fidelity and happiness. It is believed that the ducks die of sadness if separated. Mandarin ducks figure in a famous old folk poem of the Han dynasty, which tells the tragic story of a man and wife separated by his mother's constant complaints. Rather than marry others, the couple commits suicide. The families bury the tragic pair in a common grave:

> Buried them together on the side of the Hua Shan.
> To east and west they planted cypress and pine,
> To left and right they sowed the *wu-tong.*
> The trees prospered; they roofed the tomb with shade,
> Bough with bough, leaf with leaf entwined;
> And on the boughs are two flying birds
> Who named themselves Birds of True Love [mandarin ducks].
> They lift their heads and face to face they sing
> Every night till the fifth watch is done.[5]

[5]Ch'en Shou-yi, *Chinese Literature: An Historical Introduction* (New York: Ronald Press, 1961), pp. 140–41.

GOLDFISH

Lively and delicate, the Chinese goldfish symbolizes wealth and good fortune because its name, *jin-yu*, sounds like "gold in abundance." The goldfish design, with large eyes and graceful tail, is often used on ceramics and embroidery, particularly double-sided embroidery.

PEACOCK

The peacock, with its gorgeous finery, is associated with official rank. The tail feathers – always rare and highly valued – were used as a sign of rank beginning in the Ming dynasty.

Motifs and Symbols in Chinese Art continues on page 73.

COLOR PLATES

Hand-crafted vase of white and green jadeite, flower and bird motif. From Shanghai.

Opposite, top: Guangdong's distinctive ivory carving – flower basket with goldfish. *Opposite, bottom:* The "Weaving Maid and Herd Boy" legend is depicted in an ivory carving from Guangdong Province. The ivory ball floating among the clouds has 36 layers carved by the hollowing-out method, so that while all layers are completely encased, each can revolve freely. *Above, left:* Peacock vase carved of translucent stone. The vase and flexible-link chain are carved from a single piece. A product of Qingtian in Zhejiang Province. *Above, right:* Double-handled porcelain vase, hand-painted in painstaking detail. From China's renowned porcelain center at Jingdezhen.

Top: Bronze "Galloping Steed and Flying Swallow" from Henan Province. This piece is a replica of the now world famous casting that dates to the Eastern Han dynasty (25 BC- AD 221) and was unearthed in Gansu Province in 1969. The work depicts a galloping horse with one of his hooves poised on a low-flying swallow. *Bottom:* Stone-carved basket of flowers from Zhejiang Province. Note how the artisan utilized the natural coloration of the materials to create the effect of red peony blossoms on the right side of the piece. *Opposite:* Intricate cloisonné and gold-plated tripod incense burner, inlaid with jade and semiprecious stones. Note the cloud pattern cloisonné work on the lid, created by soldering copper wires on the metal base and then baking enamel pastes into the partitions (*cloisons*). Produced in a modern workshop, Beijing.

Opposite: Embroidered silk curtain with dragon and phoenix motifs from Shanghai. The Chinese dragon is a symbol of strength and beauty while the phoenix, a supernatural creature like the dragon, represents peace and prosperity. In ancient times, these motifs were embroidered only on robes of the imperial family, the dragon for the emperors and the phoenix for the empresses. *Above:* Lacquerware plate carved with basket of flowers, Beijing. The distinctive red color is achieved by mixing sap from the lac tree with a pigment derived from cinnabar.

Left, top: Bamboo canisters and vase from Hunan Province. Bamboo carving has been an active handicraft for over one hundred years. The surface of the bamboo is smoothed and a small amount of redwood is added before carving is begun. The shape of these bamboo wares is always kept simple and tasteful. *Left, bottom:* Charming silk toys, designed as elements for a mobile, are the product of Guangdong Province. *Right:* Chinese silk flowers, a craft of relatively recent origins, have become popular throughout the world. Note the subtly lifelike quality.

DEER

Because of a play on words, deer (*lu* 鹿) also represents official salary (*lu* 禄). The deer, especially the spotted variety, is also an emblem of longevity, because it is said to be the only animal which can find the *ling-zhi* fungus of immortality.

TAO-TIE MOTIF

The *tao-tie* mask is a design containing two zoomorphic patterns meeting at a central ridge. The ridge represents the animal's nose and is flanked by a raised eye on either side. The *tao-tie* is most commonly seen on early bronzes.

Modern archeologists have not been able to trace the origin of the *tao-tie* pattern, which has endless variations and is the most common and distinctive motif of early bronzes. A tiger or dragon – or a combination of the two – may have been the inspiration for this monster mask. The design was possibly used to frighten away evil spirits.

SYMBOLS DERIVED FROM NATURAL ELEMENTS

These symbols are most frequently seen in borders or backgrounds, or as separations between different areas of decoration, such as on the base or collar of a porcelain vase.

MOUNTAINS

From earliest times mountains have been considered sacred in China. A symbol of strength, durability, and prominence, the mountain was considered to be the essence of *yang,* the masculine force in nature, and the center of powerful natural forces. Emperors came to the mountains to pay homage to heaven and eventually to gain the power immanent in the mountain. The complement of the mountain was water, representing *yin* or feminine aspects of pliancy and darkness. Together, mountain and stream were considered to represent the two complementary forces which engendered the whole range of physical configurations. The term "mountains and waters" (*shan-shui*) is in fact the term for landscape.

The mountain is also associated in early legends with a fantastic paradise of jade trees, golden fruit, mineral landscape, and wonderful animals, thought to be located in the western realm of Xi Wang Mu.

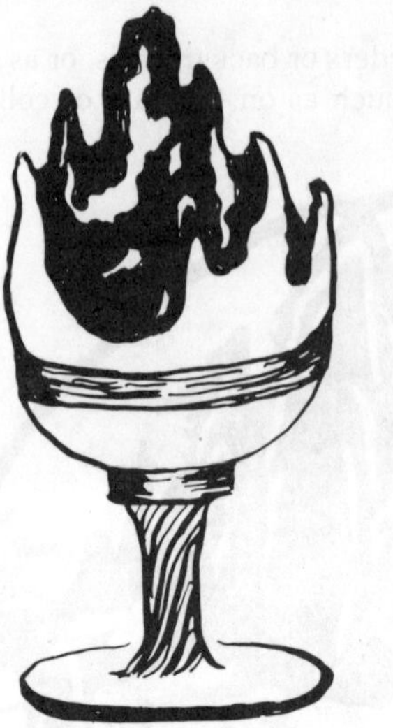

THREE ISLANDS OF
THE IMMORTALS

Situated in the Eastern Ocean, the legendary Three Islands of the Immortals were peopled with faery beings and Daoist immortals, cranes and deer, strange and wonderful trees of gold and jade, and herbs and plants of immortality, such as the *ling-zhi* fungus. The paradise is often seen on Han incense burners, and painted on lacquer and ceramics.

SUN

Usually pictured as a disc containing a three-legged crow, the red sun is a symbol of the *yang* or masculine force of nature, as well as an imperial symbol.

MOON

Just as the sun was considered to be the solidified essence of the masculine forces of nature, so the moon was seen as the crystallization of the feminine element of nature. The moon was often pictured as a disc in which a jade rabbit pounded magical ingredients to form the elixir of immortality.

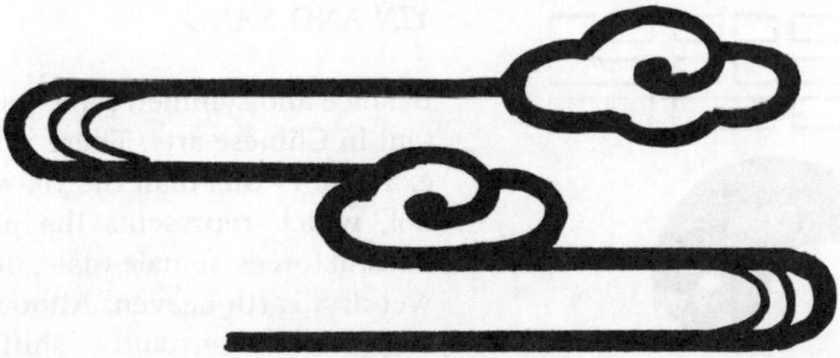

CLOUDS

An ancient symbol dating back to the earliest Chinese crafts, the cloud pattern is often used in conjunction with the dragon, who controlled the rain. Ancient forms of the symbol are simple spirals. Later, scrolls of clouds and cloud collars became conventional symbols found in most crafts, from ceramics and carving to textiles, lacquer, and cloisonné.

THUNDER

A spiral or key-shaped motif, usually linked to form a line, is seen on ancient bronzes and crafts of the Shang and Zhou dynasties. The thunder symbol has been one of the most popular geometric motifs, used on many crafts throughout the centuries–on robe borders and sleeves, on porcelain vase panels, and as a background for florals or other motifs. The basic squared spiral has many variations.

WAVES

Used in ceramics, bronzes, and textiles, the wave pattern signified the edge of the human world and the border of the Three Islands of the Immortals or the watery realm of the dragon. Waves with sun and clouds appeared as a band on porcelain plates or vases and especially as a border on court robes.

YIN AND *YANG*

Balance and symmetry are very important in Chinese arts. There is no better example of this than the *yin-yang* symbol, which represents the pairing of natural forces: female-male, dark-light, wet-dry, earth-heaven. Although these forces are constantly shifting and changing, they move together in harmony. The *yin-yang* symbol is frequently arranged with the eight trigrams in a circle around it.

SWASTIKA

An auspicious symbol of great antiquity, the swastika is part of the artistic heritage of many countries. The symbol was used in Buddhist art to indicate the number 10,000 – the eternity of the Buddha's teachings. It is possible that the swastika is related to the *chang,* or endless knot, one of the Eight Buddhist Symbols. The design is frequently used on embroidery and porcelain.

LING-ZHI

Legends say that the *ling-zhi,* or sacred fungus, brought immortality to those who ate it. Only the deer could locate the fungus, which was thought to grow high in the mountains and on the Three Islands of the Immortals. The *ling-zhi* motif is seen on ceramics and textiles, frequently grouped with the crane, pine, peach, and tortoise, the other symbols of longevity.

NUMBERED SYMBOLS

Certain objects appear as numbered groups, such as the popular craft motifs of plum blossom, pine, and bamboo (the Three Friends) or the five bats. A few others are listed here.

EIGHT TRIGRAMS

Said to be the invention of the legendary hero Fu Xi, the eight trigrams are a system of signs which represent the forces of nature. Each trigram contains three lines, each of which may be either broken or unbroken. Broken lines represent *yin* forces–passivity, feminity, darkness–while solid lines represent *yang* forces–activity, masculinity, and brightness. The trigrams were used in ancient divination, but later became a decorative motif used in bronze, porcelain, and other media.

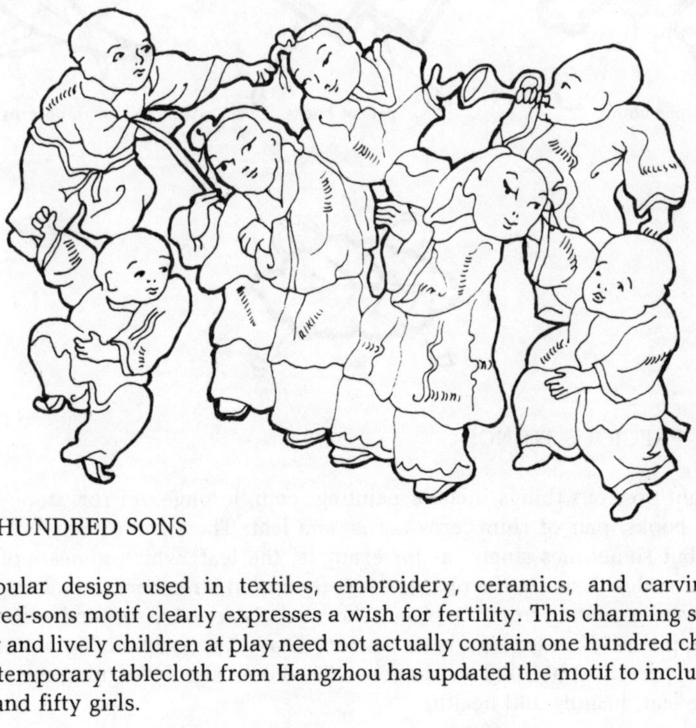

ONE HUNDRED SONS

A popular design used in textiles, embroidery, ceramics, and carving, the hundred-sons motif clearly expresses a wish for fertility. This charming scene of happy and lively children at play need not actually contain one hundred children. A contemporary tablecloth from Hangzhou has updated the motif to include fifty boys and fifty girls.

painting

coin

lozenge

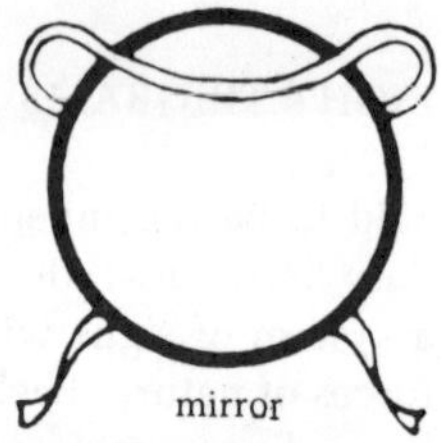

mirror

stone chime

pair of books

pair of rhinoceros horns

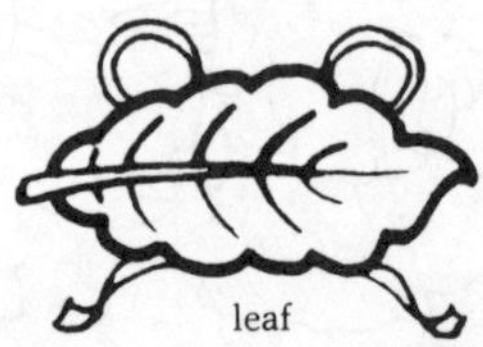

leaf

EIGHT PRECIOUS THINGS

The eight precious things include painting, coin, lozenge, mirror, stone chime, pair of books, pair of rhinoceros horns, and leaf. The signs usually occur as a group but sometimes singly, as for example, the leaf, which appears often on Qing ceramics. Usually the objects sport flying red streamers, which represent the power emanating from the piece. The symbols are all associated with wealth and happiness. The lozenge is an ancient headdress symbolizing victory; the mirror represents unbroken marital bliss. The books signify learning and culture, and the leaf, healing and health.

wheel of the law

conch

umbrella

canopy

lotus

vase

pair of fish

endless knot

EIGHT BUDDHIST SYMBOLS

Often seen on Buddhist altar implements and temple friezes, the eight religious symbols are the wheel of the law, conch, umbrella, canopy, lotus, vase, pair of fish, and endless knot. As a decorative motif the group is also seen on lacquer, ceramics, and cloisonné. Each of the Eight Buddhist Symbols has a different meaning. The most popular are the lotus – purity and faithfulness; the pair of fish – marital bliss and fidelity; and the endless knot – eternity.

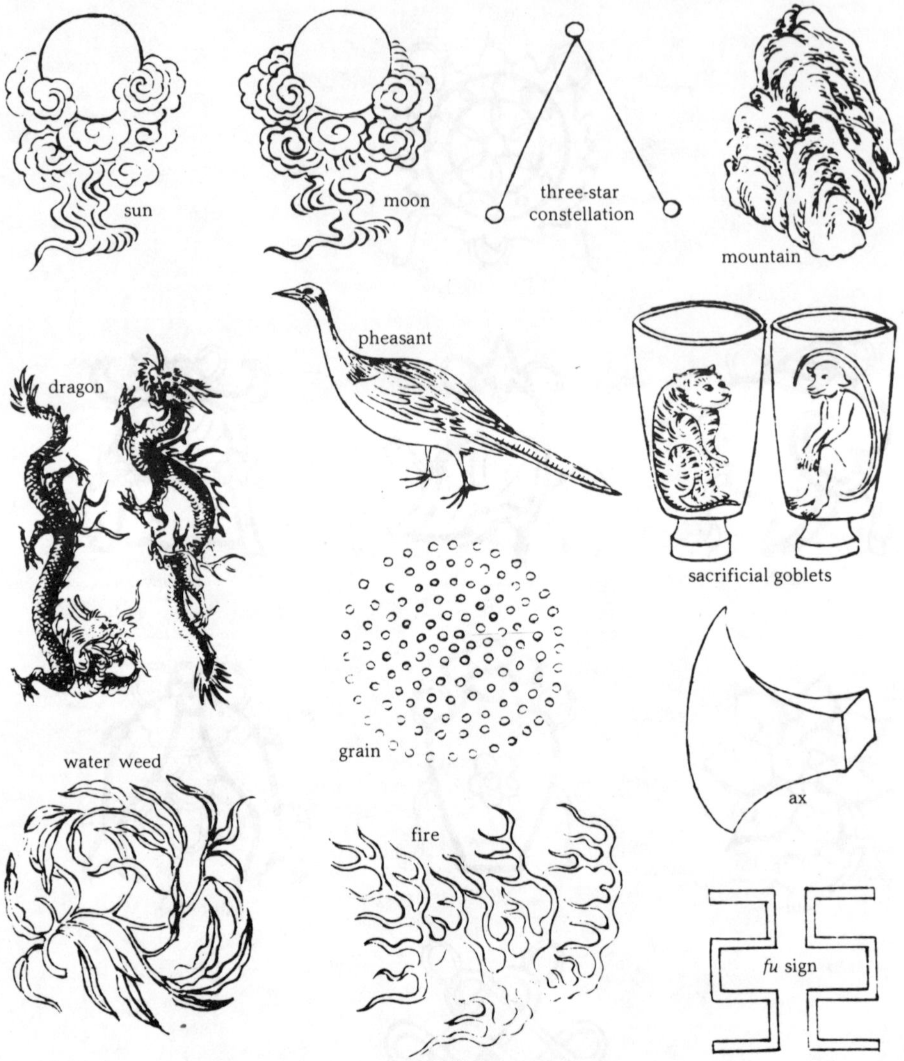

TWELVE SYMBOLS OF AUTHORITY

Of great antiquity, the twelve symbols of authority may occur alone, but are most frequently grouped together, especially on the robes of emperors and officials. Together they take on tremendous significance, representing the universe in microcosm. The symbols and their meanings include: sun, moon, and three-star constellation (heaven); mountain (earth); dragon (water, adaptability, and emperor); pheasant (literary excellence, empress); sacrificial goblets (filial piety); water weed (purity); grain (care for the people); fire (brilliance); ax (power of punishment); and *fu* sign (power of judgment).

The two final symbols were for the exclusive use of the emperor, representing his power to judge and to punish his subjects. The symbols are also associated with the five elements, five directions, and five seasons.

MONKEY

Strong, restless, ingenious, mercurial, and incorrigible, Monkey has been a favorite folk hero for centuries in China. Named Sun Wukong ("aware of the emptiness of all things"), Monkey is a character from the Ming dynasty novel *Journey to the West.* Audiences at the Beijing opera have been delighted with his exploits, such as stealing the peaches of immortality from heaven. In one opera, *Havoc in Heaven,* Monkey wears the yellow robes of the emperor, an exceedingly irreverent bit of costuming. Despite the resistance of the Jade Emperor and his spirit forces, Monkey always emerges victorious.

SHOU LAO

The aged and kindly Shou Lao, God of Longevity, is usually depicted riding on a spotted deer, surrounded by *ling-zhi* and the peaches of immortality. Sometimes he is pictured emerging from a peach, or carrying a walking stick with the head of a dragon.

XI WANG MU

The Royal Mother of the West, Xi Wang Mu, was believed to live in a paradise realm in the Western Kunlun Mountains. The peaches of longevity, as well as fantastic trees of jade and gold, grew in her country. She is often pictured riding on a crane.

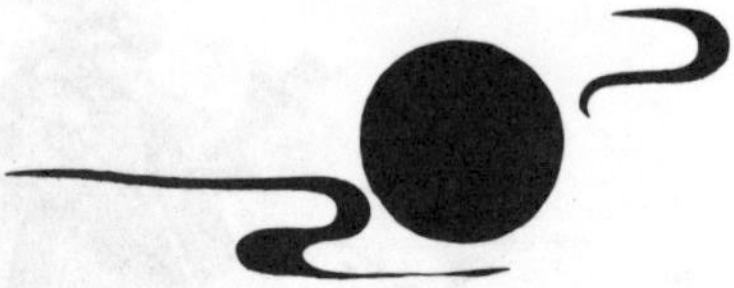

CHANG E

Legend has it that Chang E, the moon goddess, stole the drug of immortality from her husband, who ordered her death. Chang E consumed the elixir, however, and flew to the moon. Some say she was transformed into a toad with three feet, while others contend that she lives in her moon palace to this day.

In modern crafts Chang E's flight is reversed: she flies down to earth to admire all the wonderful changes that have taken place.

Chinese written symbols can be traced back at least five thousand years to pictographs on Neolithic pottery. In the Shang dynasty writing was carved on the ox bones and tortoise shells used by diviner-priests to predict future events. Originally the divination involved drilling small pits into the bone or shell and then heating the material until cracks appeared. Diviners then "read" the cracks to provide answers to their questions. The Chinese use of writing, thus, was from its inception a sacred and exclusive technique, and these characteristics have never been entirely lost.

SHUANG-XI, SYMBOL
OF SHARED BLISS

FU, SYMBOL
OF GOOD FORTUNE

SHOU, SYMBOL
OF LONGEVITY

SHUANG-XI, SYMBOL
OF SHARED BLISS

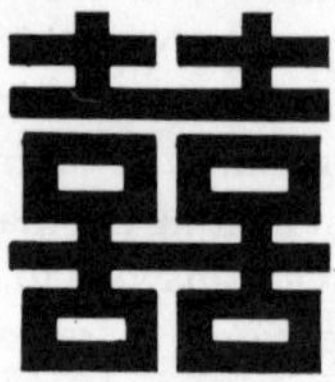

FOR FURTHER READING

Cammann, Schuyler. *Substance and Symbol in Chinese Toggles.* Philadelphia: University of Pennsylvania Press, 1962.

Hansford, S.H. *A Glossary of Chinese Art and Archeology.* London: China Society, 1954.

Medley, Margaret. *A Handbook of Chinese Art.* New York: Harper and Row, 1964.

Sze, Mai-mai, trans. *The Mustard Seed Garden Manual of Painting.* Princeton, NJ: Princeton University Press, 1963.

Williams, C.A.S. *Outlines of Chinese Symbolism and Art Motives.* New York: Dover, 1976.

PART II

THE CRAFTS

Celadon master Lai Zijiang imparts his skill to an apprentice, Longquan

CHAPTER 4

POTTERY AND PORCELAIN

MOLDING AND MODELING: THE POTTER'S ART

The basic ingredient of pottery is clay, which is malleable, sensuous, and responsive to the artist's touch. In China the earliest modeled shapes found in widespread Neolithic sites were both useful and beautiful: a basin with a fish painted on it, a water jar with flower petals on the rim. In a recently excavated Neolithic site the kilns and work place were set apart from the residential area, suggesting the importance of pottery and the existence of pottery specialists even at this early date. Down through the centuries craftsmen, sculptors, and artists have continually experimented with clay mixtures, colors, glazes, and shapes to bring ceramics to the level of a major art form. From the painted pottery of the New Stone Age to the breathtaking Ming porcelains five thousand years later, beauty, technology, and consummate skill are fused, creating objects which satisfy both practical needs and a basic human aesthetic urge. Pottery was China's first art form, and it has continued to occupy an important position up to the present.

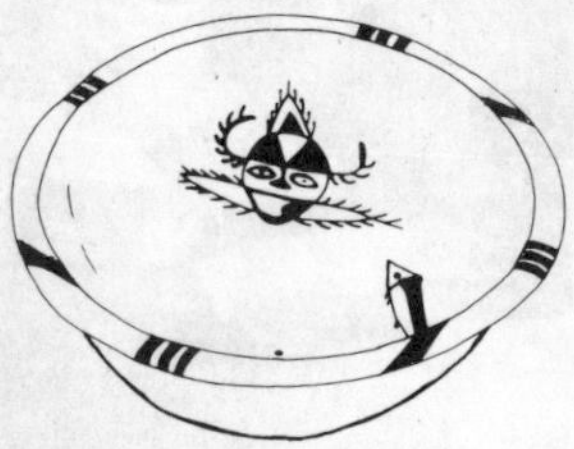

Neolithic basin with fish design

THE MAGIC OF POTTERY

Chinese legends trace the origins of pottery to the mythical hero of popular culture, Shen-nong, who is also credited with the development of agriculture, animal husbandry, and commerce. It is said that the legendary emperor Yu Di Shun greatly valued pottery and made fine pieces himself. And according to early historical accounts, the founder of the Zhou dynasty gave one of his relatives in marriage to the foremost potter of the time and honored him with the rank of prince. Although such legends are of questionable historical value, they do reveal the respect traditionally accorded to the ceramic art. The ancient Chinese rulers and noblemen paid careful attention to the clay vessels used in sacrificial rites, special celebrations, and daily activities, and skilled potters were held in high esteem.

There has always been something magical about the

Archeologists and commune workers cleaning newly discovered Neolithic pottery

Dragon plate

ceramic process. In the Han dynasty, Daoist alchemists claimed they had discovered how to transmute cinnabar (mercuric sulphide) into gold. Cinnabar was said to confer longevity on those who ate from vessels made from the refined product. Exactly what type of wares were produced is uncertain, but it is very probable that these alchemists, with their far-ranging investigations of metals, stones, and heating processes, made great contributions to ceramic techniques, even if the processes were not clearly described or understood. In the seventh century potters claimed to have created vessels of "false jade" in the furnace heat. Fine ceramics, especially celadons and porcelains, were often ranked by their similarity to jade – smoothness, luster, impermeability, and resonance. It is thus no accident that green ceramic wares, such as Yue ware and celadons, have always been highly prized in China.

Although potters had some understanding of the processes involved in firing pottery, many of the heat changes were considered somewhat magical as, for example, when variations in kiln conditions produced different colors or mottled effects. There are also many strange stories of objects which changed shape in the furnace fires or acquired special properties, such as the ability to preserve food or produce lovely music. It was said that celadon vessels cracked if poisoned food was placed in them. Such were the tall tales of Chinese pottery.

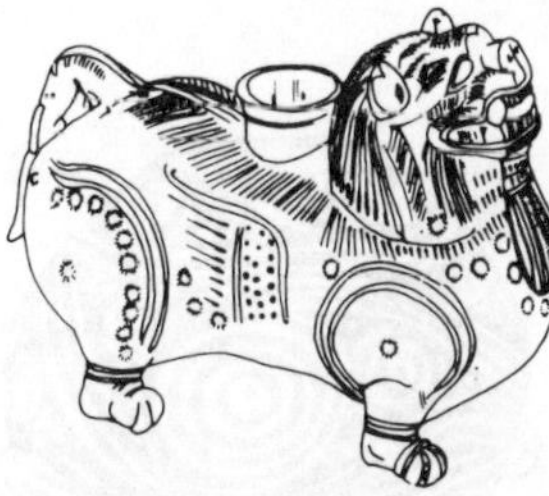

Ceramic green ware water pot

THE SECRET OF PORCELAIN

For many centuries the secret of making porcelain was known only in China. Increasing demand for Chinese porcelain in Europe during the seventeenth century led to feverish attempts to discover the secret, but it was not until the eighteenth century that the first European porcelains were produced in Dresden. Until this time Chinese ceramics dominated markets in Southeast Asia, the Near East, Africa, and Europe. Thus the ancient village craft became a thriving industry, replacing superstition with careful empirical techniques.

By the Ming dynasty, vast quantities of pottery were required both for daily use and as art wares: rice bowls, wash basins, food containers, implements for the scholar's desk such as inkstones, brush rests, and paper weights, snuff jars, water droppers, and table screens, to name a few. Ritual objects such as libation cups, incense burners, and statues were also an important category of ceramic ware. Ceramics were used in architectural decoration in the form of colored and glazed roof tiles, finials, and pierced window screens. In addition, there was a special aesthetic connected with ceramic flower vases, and special shapes and decors were to be used with certain flowers or in certain seasons. For example, a *mei-ping* vase was made to hold a single spray of plum blossom.

Modern ceramic ware

Today ceramic wares figure high among China's export goods. Thriving production centers at Liling, Shiwan, Jingdezhen, Handan, and Tangshan are producing a wide variety of art wares and articles for daily use. Pierced window screens and glazed pottery figures for roof ridges and eaves are still being made. China's fine tradition of magnificent art ceramics, such as figurines and animals, table screens, and reproductions of ancient wares, also continues today.

THE STORY OF CHINESE POTTERY

Neolithic painted pottery

Ceramic art in China stretches back some ten thousand years or more into remote prehistory. The earliest Chinese pottery discovered to date is the Neolithic painted pottery of the Yang-shao culture, dating back six thousand years. Among the pieces excavated are thin, handmade ceramic pots and vessels decorated with fish, frogs, and deer; later artifacts are covered with scrolls, swirls, and geometric patterns. Elegant burnished black vessels fashioned on a fast wheel characterize the four-thousand-year-old Long-shan culture, whose artifacts were first unearthed in Shandong. A number of shapes used in Neolithic pottery herald the forms seen later in Shang bronzes, such as the *li*, or hollow-legged tripod cauldron, the *ding*, a round bowl supported by three legs, as well as goblets and wine cups. These vessels attest to the technical skill of late Stone Age potters, who used amazingly advanced kiln technology to create shapes and designs basic to Chinese ceramic art through the succeeding millennia. Because of their virtuosity and imagination, Neolithic potters were certainly the dominant creative force of the age.

Ceramic tripod pitcher with hollow legs

Archeologists piecing together a Neolithic ceramic tripod

CONTRIBUTIONS OF THE SHANG AND ZHOU

During the Shang (ca. 1700–1066 BC) and Zhou (ca. 1066–256 BC), bronze became the outstanding artistic medium. The potter's skill was revealed in the creation of the ceramic molds in which ritual bronze vessels were cast. Every angle and relief, every line and curve of the finished bronze was first formed in a ceramic mold. This, the potter's contribution to the formation of Shang and Zhou bronzes, has been often overlooked.

Even at this early date the Shang potter was experimenting with clay mixtures and firing processes that would eventually lead to the production of porcelain. Observing that some pots acquired a glossy finish when wood ash fell on them during the firing process, Shang potters were able to reproduce the hard, glass-like coating in kilns which reached temperatures of 1,200°C. This marked the first appearance of hard-glazed ceramics. The Shang also made beautiful "early stoneware" out of a white clay called kaolin. These brittle, finely shaped vessels, often bearing incised designs similar to those on Shang bronzes, preceded the true porcelain of the Tang by two thousand years.

BURIAL CUSTOMS AND TOMB FIGURES

Like many ancient civilizations, the early Chinese believed in a very concrete afterlife. Hence the dead were buried with all the furnishings, utensils, and comforts to which they were accustomed in life. This belief, which can be traced back at least to the Shang, created a demand for skilled artisans in every craft to re-create all the objects of practical value and beauty which sovereign and noble would need in the afterworld.

During the Shang, living slaves were buried in the tomb of the ruler and nobility, so they could have

Qin pottery figures

proper attendants in death as in life. In the Zhou, figurines modeled of straw, clay, or wood were fashioned to replace the human retainers. This change spurred the development of terra-cotta sculpture. Most of the sculpture has come to light only in the twentieth century; digging and construction on roads and railroads, as well as systematic archeological investigation, have led to the discovery of hundreds of ancient tombs. These excavations show that by the third century BC ceramic sculpture was already quite advanced in China. Recent discoveries in Shaanxi Province near the tomb of the first Qin emperor, who was buried in 210 BC, revealed an army of over seven thousand life-size, realistically sculpted terra-cotta warriors, fully clad in armor and accompanied by fierce war horses and battle chariots.

"Ming-qi" and Han Realism

The small, clay burial figures were called *ming-qi.* These funerary utensils were modeled by hand or made in shallow molds, then painted and finished individually by the potter after firing. Modeled with great concern for detail, these pieces chronicle the emergence of a realistic art style, traceable to the third or fourth century BC. While sophisticated bronze casting continued during the Han, the freer forms of the new realism reflected the changing spirit of this cosmopolitan age. The Han ruled over a far-flung empire; trade routes led to the Near East via the Silk Road and to Annam (North Viet Nam) in Southeast Asia. The increased traffic and foreign contacts were a creative impetus to the innovative Han craftsman, as was the Han system of patronage provided by the nobility and wealthy merchants.

An extensive pottery industry evolved, in part to fill the tremendous demand for *ming-qi.* Indeed, from the first to the third century AD, such large quantities of burial figures were needed that imperial workshops in the capital and provinces began mass-production to satisfy the demand. Most craftsmen worked in these imperial factories.

The objects buried in Han tombs reflect the whole range of furnishings and implements actually used in the homes of the wealthy upper classes of the day. The *ming-qi* provide an insight into the great variety of Han life, from multistoried houses of elaborate design to farms and pigsties, from elegant ladies and lively musicians to dogs, bears, and galloping horses. The artisan's goal was to create objects so lifelike that they would continue to exist in the afterworld much as they existed in life. Horses are caught seemingly in mid-gallop, ready to spring away at royal command.

Even the Daoist paradise was conceived in a realistic, physical manner, as in the hill jars and incense burners shaped like mountainous islands rising from lapping waves, encircled by patterns of animals and birds. Warring States and Early Han tombs also contained pottery forms borrowed from bronzes, such as the *hu* wine jar, in which the pottery vessel was glazed, carved, molded, or painted with geometric patterns to imitate the bronze originals.

Ceramic pig, Han dynasty

Burial Figures Under the Tang

Vigorous realism reappeared in the brilliant polychrome *(san-cai)* burial figures of the Tang dynasty (618–907). These sculptures depicting camels carrying sheep, chickens, and silks in their packs, elegantly haughty court ladies, proud horses with arched necks, fearsome tomb guardians, and foreign travelers modeled in a style verging on caricature provide a delightful view of cosmopolitan Tang life. Tang protocol determined the quantity and size of such funerary wares, depending upon the deceased's rank as prince, prime minister, or official. According to the customs of the time, burial objects were displayed in the dead man's home and then exhibited as part of the funeral cortege, in order to make a dazzling display of the wealth and status of the departed. In the prosperous times of the early Tang, funerals became increasingly lavish, and the art of *ming-qi* reached its zenith. The artists who breathed life into these figures were sculptors of the highest order, working from one commission to the next. It is certain that the best workshops and sculptors were in great demand.

Horse in three color pottery

In Xian, Luoyang, and other ancient cities where ceramic workshops existed centuries ago, ceramicists are today meticulously re-creating treasures from the Han and Tang, using the techniques of the past in combination with modern tools. Present-day replicas are of extremely high quality and can be found in museum shops and Friendship Stores in major cities throughout China.

FROM EARTHENWARE TO GREEN WARE

Much of Han pottery is earthenware covered with a low-fired lead glaze. Numerous samples of earthenware jars made of red or gray clay with iron-rich olive or brown glazes have been discovered in Han tombs, as well as unglazed pottery painted in white, red, or black pigments. Decorations in low relief under the glaze often depicted "the hunt among mountains," with dragons, birds, animals, and hunters engaged in an energetic circular chase around the vessel.

Yue Ware

Ewer of Yue ware, Six Dynasties period

At the same time high-fired feldspathic wares were being manufactured. These appeared during the Warring States period and became more common during the Han. Potters continued to search for ways to create artificial jade. Pale green Yue ware was made at numerous centers in Zhejiang province. Resembling jade in luminosity, these lovely early celadons were to maintain a place of continuous distinction in Chinese ceramics. Simple and elegantly shaped basins, bowls, and jars covered with glossy rich glazes of soft gray-green or brown are characteristic of the Yue ware produced from the first century until well into the seventh century. Lamp bases or water jugs were commonly shaped into sheep, bears, birds, or lions. As potters developed better control of their kilns, glazes became more even in color and the clay bodies grew more refined, foreshadowing the splendid celadons of the Song.

Celadons: Ceramic Jade

Reproduction of ancient celadon

In the fourteenth century, a sea-going junk on its way to Japan sank during a storm near the coast of Korea. In 1978 when the wreck was excavated, the largest collection of ceramics outside China was found, and most of these pieces turned out to be celadons. Chinese celadons have been found on South Sea beaches, in Philippine jungles, Arabian palaces, and among East African ruins. During the Song dynasty (960–1279), they were the major pottery exported to Southeast Asia and the Pacific; when they reached Europe in the Ming dynasty (1368–1644), celadons became all the rage. In the French play *L'Astrée*, produced in 1610, the shepherd boy named Céladon wore ribbons of the same gray-green color as this ware, and the name was subsequently connected with this beautiful green pottery from China.

The Chinese prized celadons for their color, which was said to resemble "the tones of the distant hills," "the soft jade-green of onion sprouts in autumn," "a wet, mossy bank," or "slender willow twigs." Celadons resemble precious jade in luster and tone, and it is probable that Daoist alchemists were searching for ways to create artificial jade when Yue ware was first produced. Not surprisingly, during the Song and Yuan dynasties the best and most numerous wares came from Longquan, near the site of the ancient Yue ware kilns.

Longquan celadons were decorated with relief motifs of clouds and lotus petals under a thick, smooth, green glaze which shone with a rich luster. This was a time of misty landscape paintings and celebration of the past, owing to renewed interest in Confucianism. Celadons were sometimes fashioned in the shapes of ancient bronzes. Imperial Ge ware from Longquan, with a crackled glaze, were tinted in every imaginable shade of green. The shapes were pure, classic, and subtle, appealing to the refined aesthetics of the Song court. Legends say that two brothers named Zhang set up kilns, the younger brother producing Longquan celadons, and the elder brother (*ge* in Chinese) founding his own kilns using crackle glazes. Crackle ware later became a favorite of the Song court.

Celadon ewer

Hangzhou commune where world-famous Longjing Tea is produced

A Pot for the Tea

The great popularity of tea drinking in the Tang dynasty brought a growing demand for exquisite tea utensils and a formal approach to the preparation and consumption of tea. Certain wares were most valued for their

Retired tea cultivators

enhancement of the color and flavor of tea. Green wares were ranked the highest by the eighth century writer Lu Yu, who wrote the *Classic of Tea*, an important work which set standards of taste for centuries. Pure, thin, white wares were also prized. By the Ming dynasty tea cups from Jingdezhen were such a vogue at court that concerned ministers, braving death, criticized the imperial practice of ordering new sets almost daily.

Elegant Dehua teapot, Ming dynasty

Tea cups and pots became an important element of Chinese ceramic history because the social life of scholars and nobility of the Tang and Song dynasties revolved around teahouses, where gentlemen met to be entertained by female musicians and performers, enjoy the company of friends, and compose poetry. Tea drinking, which had been introduced into China several centuries before, now required prescribed utensils and became a serious hobby for scholars and monks who valued the beverage for its gentle stimulation and association with the pleasures of congenial companions. A Song stoneware came to be greatly admired by the Japanese for use in their tea ceremony. Called *temmoku* in Japanese, this ware from Fujian had a rich black glaze with marks known as 'hare's fur' and 'oil spots.' The development of celadons and porcelain brought new Chinese wares to accommodate the overwhelming enthusiasm for tea, but by the Ming, Yixing stoneware teapots, small and round, frequently modeled in the shape of a gourd, were considered to be without equal.

Modern red glazed teapot, Shiwan

Blue-and-white porcelain vase with imperial dragon

PORCELAIN: THE PINNACLE OF CHINESE CERAMICS

Marco Polo was the first European to record the Chinese process of porcelain production. Although some of the details were inaccurate, his overall impression was correct:

> Of this place there is nothing further to be observed, than that cups or bowls and dishes of porcelainware are there manufactured. The process was explained to be as follows. They collect a certain kind of earth, as it were, from a mine, and laying it in a great heap, suffer it to be exposed to the wind, the rain, and the sun, for thirty or forty years, during which time it is never disturbed. By this it becomes refined and fit for being wrought into the vessels above mentioned. Such colours as may be thought proper are then laid on, and the ware is afterwards baked in ovens or furnaces.[1]

During the cosmopolitan age of the Tang, continued experimentation with ceramic techniques led to perfection of the true porcelain so prized for drinking tea.

The Song court reserved for its use the most perfect and elegant monochromes and white wares. Porcelain was now translucent, resonant, and thin-bodied, like the green-tinged, white ding ware – a *guan*, or official, ceramic designated for use by the court.

Porcelain Guan-yin, Dehua

To Westerners, the Ming dynasty is synonymous with porcelain. To this day the word "Ming" still evokes visions of beautiful blue dragons coiling around a white porcelain urn. By the seventeenth century porcelains were known all over the world. In Europe palaces were built with "porcelain rooms," and no king or emperor was without his own collection of these precious wares,

[1] Manuel Komroff, ed., *The Travels of Marco Polo* (New York: Modern Library, 1953), pp. 255–56.

which fitted so well with the European rococco art style. Philip II of Spain, for example, had some three thousand pieces in his private collection. However, Europe did not discover the secret formula of porcelain until the early eighteenth century, a thousand years after its development in China.

The Age of Porcelain

Porcelain vase with blue-and-white underglaze, Yuan dynasty

During the Ming the technique of underglaze painting in cobalt blue and copper red, which had evolved during the Song and Yuan dynasties, came close to perfection. The blue-and-white ceramics were the most popular wares at first, but more colorful polychromes with enamel overglaze soon gained favor. The Ming potter used many varieties of decor: delicate and transparent overglaze enamel painting, enamel glazes, glazes over carved slips (coatings), and combinations of carving and painting. Bold florals with vivid glazes reminiscent of the Tang presented a sharp contrast to the refined and understated wares of the Song.

The Ming court spurred potters on to creative triumph in porcelain refinement. In the fourteenth century the first Ming emperor designated special kilns in Jingdezhen for production of imperial wares, and soon the town became the most important pottery center in China. Known as the Porcelain Capital of the World, this small city in the remote hills of Jiangxi Province made porcelain for the court, for growing domestic needs, and for export all over the world.

Qing Dynasty Ceramics

Porcelains of this era have been described as the perfection of style, shape, glaze, and decoration. Imperial wares from the Song and Ming were reproduced at Jingdezhen. The potters of Jingdezhen had become so skillful that they could easily imitate all the wares of previous centuries and simulate wood, ivory, jade, and other effects in a ceramic medium. Qing innovations included copper red glazes, from blush pink and crushed strawberry to deep red oxblood, and the use of new translucent colors in enamel painting, such as "famille verte" and later "famille rose." The latter, called *yang-cai* or "foreign color" by the Chinese, derived its tone from gold and was probably introduced by Jesuits at the Qing court. "Famille rose" wares also revealed Western influence in the use of shading techniques seen in Western painting. By the eighteenth century Jingdezhen was supplying most of the porcelain for export.

Snuff bottles, Qing dynasty

Merchant groups had an increasingly important position and dictated the porcelain designs of hundreds of commercial kilns.

During the nineteenth century, designs became more and more elaborate. Often, entire pieces were covered with enamel painting and were threaded with gold, in imitation of embroidery. Pierced openwork revealed the potters' enormous skill, and high reliefs were intricately carved or modeled. The patterns and shapes of ancient bronzes were copied endlessly. Soon, however, endless elaboration and repetition signaled a decline in this formerly vigorous art. Moreover, the upheavals which shook all Chinese society in the late nineteenth and early twentieth centuries inevitably affected the porcelain industry, and by 1950 only a handful of kilns were operating in some areas. Most of the once great kilns were closed.

EXPORT WARES

From the seventh to the thirteenth centuries ceramics were largely exported to Southeast Asia, Japan, the Pacific, and along the Silk Road to India, Persia, and Egypt. The great quantities of celadon and white porcelain uncovered in archeological digs throughout these areas attest to the extent of this commerce, which in turn brought to China ivory, glass, and cobalt blue pigments, among other imports. Most exports to Southeast Asia were supplied by the kilns of Zhejiang and Fujian provinces, and Arab traders formed a large community in the Fujian port of Xiamen (Amoy). Tang polychromes were well-liked and imitated in Persia, and Song celadons found a ready market throughout the Arab world. The ceramic art of Japan, Korea, and Southeast Asia also showed the marked influence of Chinese exports.

By the fourteenth century fine pieces of porcelain marketed throughout Asia were being made at the kilns of Jingdezhen, and by the sixteenth century the Manila galleons of Portuguese traders were carrying porcelains to Europe. The first trade between Europe and China was in the blue-and-white wares of Jingdezhen. Vast quantities were soon being shipped to Europe, and by the late seventeenth century, European agents at Guangzhou were placing orders designed with specific decorations to suit European tastes. The kilns of Guangdong and Fujian provinces also provided export wares in the Ming and Qing periods, and export porcelains were often sent from Jingdezhen to be decorated in the port of Guangzhou.

The trade in Chinese ceramics slackened in the nineteenth century as European porcelain began to fill domestic needs. Cheap chinaware produced in Europe and America during the early twentieth century finally ended the export trade – technologically backward China could no longer compete.

CHINESE CERAMICS TODAY

Since 1949 the government of the People's Republic of China has reopened a number of old potteries and provided financial, scientific, and artistic aid. In terms of technique, rediscovery of forgotten wares and glazes, and renewal of skills, the past thirty years have been very fruitful. Today Jingdezhen in Jiangxi Province is again the most important porcelain center in China, specializing in its traditional blue-and-white underglaze porcelains. Shiwan, near Guangzhou, is once more the pottery capital of the south, and its sculpted figurines preserve an ancient art form at that kiln.

Throughout the centuries widely scattered kilns in all regions of China developed specific styles and wares, and today kilns still specialize in their traditional forms. One of the goals of modern research has been to reestablish ancient kilns and their fine pottery, even when they have been dormant for hundreds of years. Both historically and at present, however, kilns produced many different types of wares. Whenever a new technique or artistic effect became popular, other kilns throughout the country imitated the new style. Today most kiln centers are working to establish fully automated modern plants for dinnerware and other daily use ceramics, as well as fine art ware.

POTTERY AND PORCELAIN: TECHNIQUES AND MATERIALS

CLAY: THE BASIC INGREDIENT

The possibilities of a lump of clay are almost limitless. It can be used to create objects of practical use or ritual purposes, or pieces of great beauty. The techniques involved can be very simple, requiring only a potter, a lump of clay, and a small kiln, or much more complex, as in the factory system in which each piece is crafted in stages by many people. Ceramic wares may be modeled by hand, formed on a wheel, or made in a mold. The possible designs and decorations are almost limitless.

Rural potter at work

Earthenware

Earthenware is the earliest and most basic type of pottery. This type of pottery, which is still manufactured today in China, is formed of coarse, often unrefined clay mixed with sand (silica) for added strength. Earthenware is fired in a kiln at a relatively low temperature, 800°–1,000°C. The finished product is thick, porous, brittle, and easily broken. When glazed, the ware gains a hard coat which is impervious to liquids.

Stoneware

Making molds for stoneware figurines

Stoneware is created when more fusible materials, such as feldspar and quartz, are added to refined clays and then high-fired at kiln temperatures from 1,100° to 1,250°C. The result is a stronger, harder, nonporous, and vitrified ware. Although experimentation with feldspathic clays and glazes in the production of stoneware eventually led to the development of porcelain, stoneware has retained its own distinction and characteristic design. "Porcellaneous stoneware" is high-fired and fine bodied, derived from a formula close to that of porcelain. The principal difference is that stoneware is opaque, while porcelain is translucent.

Porcelain

Porcelain is a thin, hard, and translucent white ceramic made from a combination of highly refined white plastic clay called kaolin mixed in almost equal proportions with a white powder of the same basic feldspathic composition called petuntse or "China clay." The word kaolin comes from the Gaoling Hills near Jingdezhen, where this type of clay was found in vast quantity. Petuntse is derived from the Chinese term *bai*

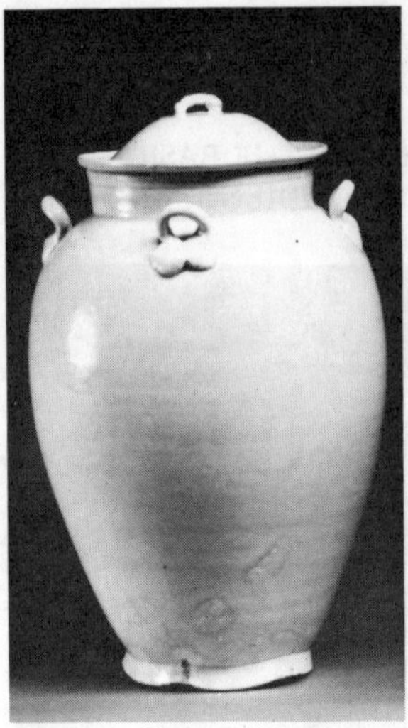

Ying-qing white porcelain, Northern Song dynasty

dun-zi, meaning "white briquettes," describing the state in which the refined white powder was received at the kiln site. Petuntse has a lower melting point than kaolin, and its addition makes kaolin less brittle. The proportion of kaolin to petuntse varies with the quality of the ceramic – the finer the porcelain, the greater the amount of kaolin used. Porcelain is glazed with a liquid mixture of the same feldspathic formula as the body and then high-fired at a kiln temperature of 1,300°C or more. At this heat, body and glaze fuse and become totally vitrified. Porcelain is the unique achievement of the Chinese potter, and indeed "china" is the Chinese ware par excellence. Porcelain is thought to have been named by Portuguese sailors after the word "porzella," a smooth, shiny cowrie shell. Porcelain has a clear ringing sound when tapped.

Bisque or Biscuit

Ceramics may be fired without a glaze, and the resulting ware is called the biscuit. High-fired without a glaze, porcelain will have a matt instead of a glossy finish. The biscuit may then be glazed or decorated with enamels requiring a lower temperature and refired. In many small figurines the faces may be left unglazed to accent the sharp modeling of the features, while the bodies are painted in glossy enamels.

Slip

Slip is a thin, liquid, clay mixture applied to the ware as a base before glazing. The mixture is "slipped" on, either to conceal defects in the color or shape of the body or to provide a base for painted decoration. Parts which have been separately molded, such as high reliefs and cup handles, are fastened (luted) to the clay body by means of a slip.

Potter's Wheel

In addition to molding or modeling the clay, a potter's wheel is used to build a form. One of the earliest human inventions, the wheel is a flat, horizontal, disc-like table, which can be spun by means of a foot pedal, thus leaving the potter's hands free to shape the spinning clay.

Kilns

The two basic types are *oxidation kilns* and *reduction kilns.* In an oxidation kiln the air is allowed to circulate freely, while the oxygen in a reduction kiln is cut off, and the oven closed as tightly as possible. The colors derived from metallic oxides vary depending on these kiln conditions. Thus iron oxides fire brown or yellow in an oxidizing atmosphere, but the same pigment turns green or blue in a closed reduction kiln. Even slightly varying conditions will produce green, lavender, gray, or turquoise. Splashy and mixed colors are achieved by varying the kiln atmosphere.

When ceramics are put into the kiln, they must be boxed to protect them from ashes and other impurities. The boxes are called "saggars," and their design demands great skill, much like mold-making, so that the vessel fits exactly within the saggar.

Dotted over the southern Chinese landscape are centuries-old "dragon kilns," tunnels built on the hillsides, each higher than the one connected below. Some had as many as ten or twelve chambers, varying from very hot to cooler temperatures, and could fire five thousand pieces of pottery at the same time. A different kiln arrangement was seen in northern China, where single kilns were placed close to each other, but not connected. These are called "beehive" kilns. Modern kilns are often computerized and continuous, making them much easier to fire, but for certain effects only the old dragon kilns will do. A muffle or enameler's kiln is used to fire at 750°-800°C, and the enameled pieces are encased for protection from the direct source of heat.

GLAZES AND COLORS

Earthenware, stoneware, and porcelain are usually embellished by the application of a glaze. Glaze is a liquid mixture applied to a clay object, producing a glossy coat after firing. Glaze may be applied with a brush, by blowing through a bamboo tube with gauze on one end, or by dipping a pottery piece in the mixture.

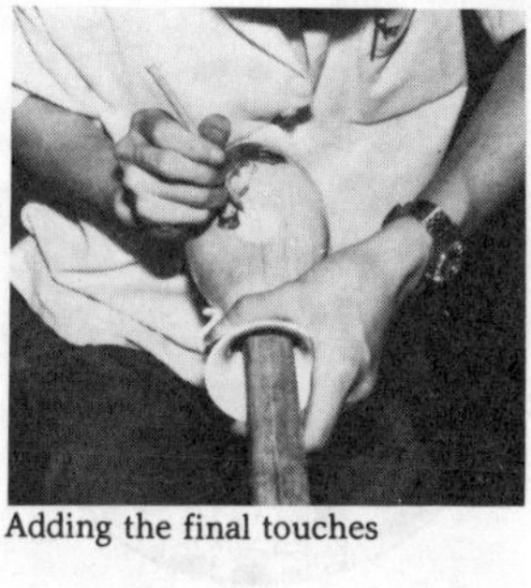
Adding the final touches

The Chinese potter can choose between a clear glaze or a glaze with color. Variegated effects such as splashed colors, mottles, streaks, and crackles are produced by the variation of metallic colorants and kiln conditions. There are two basic types of ceramic glazes: those requiring high temperature to fuse and those with a low melting point.

The Chinese potter chose from a variety of metallic pigments to create beautiful and unique ceramic works. But for high-fired glazes and underglaze painting on porcelain, only cobalt, iron, and copper oxide colorants could maintain their color at the high temperatures necessary for firing.

Modern piece from Longquan with crackle glaze

Crackle occurs in the glaze of a piece when the body and glaze cool at different rates. The crackle was probably produced at first by accident, as seen in Han dynasty stoneware, but potters learned to control the technique to produce varied effects. Such pieces were very popular in the Song, and the technique is still used in fine art pieces today.

Feldspathic or "Hard" Glazes

Feldspathic glazes requiring high temperatures to vitrify were developed very early in Chinese ceramic history. The gray-green glazes of the late Han, forerunners of the famous Song celadons, were of feldspathic composition. These are the only glazes which may be used on the raw (unfired) porcelain body. In the eighteenth century an array of beautiful colored glazes was achieved when potters completely mastered kiln conditions and temperatures.

Lead Glazes

"Soft" glazes of lead silicate (glass) are fired at low or moderate temperatures (900°C). First seen during the Warring States period, and more abundantly on Han wares, they were perfected in later dynasties. In the Tang, metallic oxides were added as colorants, producing the brilliant *san-cai* polychromes of green, white, yellow, brown, and blue. Colorful lead glazes were used during the Ming dynasty on the porcelain biscuit for wares also termed *san-cai* or, more usually, *fa-hua*. In these, slip partitions were built to separate the colors, as in cloisonné. Lead glazes on the biscuit were also popular in a variety of monotones. After application of the glaze, the porcelain piece then had to be refired.

Enamels

Enamels are similar to lead glazes in requiring a very low firing temperature, about 800°C. They can only be applied to porcelain after the object has been high-fired, and a second firing is necessary to fuse the enamel.

Early example of blue-and-white underglaze porcelain

Underglaze Painting

Underglaze painting is the technique of painting directly on a raw (unfired) porcelain body, applying a thin layer of clear glaze, and then firing. The resulting painted design appears to float between the glaze and the body, and the colors then glow through the glaze with an iridescence superior to that of any other porcelain. In addition, the underglaze technique assures that colors cannot wear off, and there is no possibility of lead poisoning.

The technique has been known since the Tang dynasty. During the Ming and Qing dynasties, the most famous Chinese underglaze was cobalt blue, called Mohammedan blue when it was first imported from the Near East. Later, deposits were discovered in China and native pigments were used. Copper oxide provided the "underglaze red" of Ming porcelains, and both colors retained their distinctive quality even after high-firing.

Large *mei-ping* vase, painted decoration in underglaze red

A beautiful family of eighteenth century glazes was the copper red group. Produced with varied amounts of copper and under varying kiln conditions, the colors ranged from a soft, pinkish-red "peach bloom" to the deep red of "oxblood" and the streaked red "flambé." The red glazes were shiny and heavy, in contrast to the many hues of the softer cobalt blues.

The soft, gray-green celadons–one of the loveliest groups of Chinese ceramics–derived their distinctive shade from iron-tinged glazes. Shiny "mirror black" was achieved with iron and a pinch of cobalt. Qing potters produced these new colored glazes by experimenting with endless mixtures of metallic oxides.

Overglaze Painting

Overglaze painting is the technique whereby enamels are applied to a glazed porcelain piece, which is then refired. This technique led to the *wu-cai* and *dou-cai* polychrome porcelains of the Ming dynasty, which combined underglaze blue with overglaze enamels. The "famille verte" and "famille rose" wares of the Qing used translucent enamel colors especially suited to porcelain painting. Copper-based green, with the addition of purple, yellow, and coral, makes up the "famille verte" palette, while rich pink derived from gold, with added colors of black, blue, yellow, and gold, makes up the "famille rose." These colors maintain their delicacy and brightness only when fired at low kiln temperatures, however. Enamels used on porcelain are exactly the same as those used for cloisonné.

DECORATION

After the fourteenth century painting provided the main source of decoration for porcelain. Colored glazes of all kinds had been a popular decorative element for stoneware and porcelain for centuries, and the "true" ceramic modes of decor are incising, carving, stamping, impressing, modeling, and molding. These are all decoration of the clay itself; along with glazing, these were considered to be the most refined and classic decor. Elegant shapes of the vessels were in themselves classic decorative elements. Celadons and other wares of the Song emphasized pure form, as well as the color, luminosity, and transparency of the glaze.

One example of a ceramic incising technique is *anhua* or "secret decoration," in which the thickly applied slip is faintly carved in a pattern often invisible except when held to the light. Many porcelains, especially in the eighteenth century, combined techniques of carving and painting. A well-known example is the "rice grain" pattern: little perforations are carved in the biscuit (like rice grains), and after underglaze painting, usually in cobalt, the piece is glazed and fired. The perforations are filled with glaze, thus forming a translucent pattern which adds to the blue-and-white decor. Other decors included elaborate high reliefs which were luted to the body, as in a teapot which sprouted a whole bamboo branch as a decoration. Pierced or open work, where the porcelain was carved completely through, was another decorative form.

Porcelain bowl with Three Friends motif, Qing dynasty

The array of motifs found in painted porcelain covers the entire repertoire of designs common to all the arts of China: the ever-present dragon appears in his many manifestations, and the "three friends"–prunus, pine, and bamboo–are seen frequently.

The Ming and Qing pottery painters were skilled in emphasizing the curves of a vase with bands of design, or framing a motif on a plate with scrolls of peonies or lotus. Rhythmic cloud or wave abstractions were sometimes painted on the collar of a vase, and the lower curve of the urn decorated with "lotus panels," a stylized leaf design which provides neat frames for a flower or other motifs. Sages and beauties are often found in porcelain landscapes. Designs were copied from other crafts and from models, but they were reinterpreted again and again with seemingly limitless individuality and variation.

THE KILNS, YESTERDAY AND TODAY

Hand-painting porcelain at Jingdezhen

O'er desert sands, o'er gulf and bay,
O'er Ganges and o'er Himalay,
Bird-like I fly, and flying sing,
To flowery kingdoms of Cathay,
And bird-like poise on balanced wing
Above the town of King-te-tching,
A burning town, or seeming so,—
Three thousand furnaces that glow
Incessantly, and fill the air
With smoke uprising, gyre on gyre,
And painted by the lurid glare,
Of jets and flashes of red fire.

"KERAMOS"
Henry Wadsworth Longfellow, 1877

JINGDEZHEN: PORCELAIN CAPITAL OF THE WORLD

The King-te-tching of Longfellow's poem was in reality Jingdezhen, the porcelain capital of China in the Ming dynasty and again today. The exquisite porcelains which graced the courts of Chinese emperors, Arabian princes, and European kings have been created in this remote city for over a thousand years. Jingdezhen is located on the banks of the Chang River in the hills of northeast Jiangxi Province. Its busy harbor is filled with riverboats unloading kaolin and petuntse from down-stream hills, then ferrying the precious finished cargo downriver and through Lake Boyang up to the Yangzi or on down to Nanchang. Until recently, overland transportation was hazardous, and no railroad existed until about six years ago. An eighteenth century missionary, Père D'Entrecolles, described Jingdezhen this way: from the harbor at night, the town looked like a vast city of flame, a great furnace smoking from its three thousand kilns. D'Entrecolles noted that the city was unwalled (*zhen*), which made security difficult, but this was necessary to permit the constant in-and-out movement of raw materials and finished goods. Strict surveillance and regulations were necessary to protect the valuable porcelains, and strangers were never permitted to sleep at Jingdezhen unless they stayed with acquaintances who would be responsible for their conduct. Poverty was widespread, and even the skilled artisans were poorly paid.

In his letters, D'Entrecolles also described how porcelain was made. It was from his copious notes that the preparation of the clays and the actual methods of production became known in Europe. The porcelains he described were made by as many as seventy workers, from mold makers to glazers. Even the painting was divided – one painter did outlines and another filled in the washes. No painter or potter signed the work. Rather, it was the collective skill and artistry of the Jingdezhen craftsmen, as seen in sculpting, carving, painting, and incising, which was renowned.

Jingdezhen received its present name in the Song dynasty when a collection of porcelain was commissioned for the court. The kilns date back at least as far as the seventh century, and both legend and recent archeological discoveries indicate a pottery center near this location as early as the first century AD. The first famous Jingdezhen wares were the fine bluish-white *qing-bai* or *ying-qing* porcelains made during the Song. During the Yuan, underglazed blue-and-white wares were first made at Jingdezhen. The pigment had probably been brought to China by Persian traders. Although local cobalt was also used, the imported pigment, called Mohammedan blue, produced a deeper, richer color.

The Ming Imperial Kilns

In 1369 the first Ming emperor set aside kilns in Jingdezhen solely for imperial use, and from that time all the porcelain for the Ming and Qing courts was supplied by these imperial kilns. The city soon eclipsed all the other potteries in China, and in the early years of trade with Europe, almost all export porcelain came from this small city as well.

In China, porcelain played a vital role in the daily life

Old kiln sites dotting the Jiangxi countryside

of the mandarin class and the growing class of urban merchants. No banquet was complete without these exquisite dishes and bowls, often celebrated in poetry, and a home without porcelain accessories was deemed poorly furnished. The imperial court alone demanded huge shipments: palace records show that one hundred thousand pieces were ordered in the year 1546. Many imperial dinner services had specified designs, and paintings were often sent to the potters by the court to be copied in porcelain.

All this production required painstaking, unremitting labor. There was discontent among the workers due to production speedups and poor working conditions. In the mid-sixteenth century a petition was sent to the court explaining that due to floods and a bad fire, frequent in this "city of fire," one sizeable order simply could not be met. The difficult and sometimes perilous working conditions are also seen in the following account. During the Ming dynasty, the court sent orders for large "dragon fishbowls," some three feet in diameter and two feet high, whose size made their production extremely difficult. After successive produc-

tion attempts failed, the eunuchs in charge of the factory meted out severe punishments to the workers. Unable to bear this bitter situation, a potter named Tong threw himself to his death in the furnace. When the dragon bowls were subsequently removed from the flames, they were found to be flawless. The workers then set up a temple to worship the dead potter and offered annual sacrifices to him.

By the end of the Ming, most porcelain techniques were thoroughly perfected. Early in the fifteenth century, "bodiless" or "eggshell" porcelain was produced, so fine and white that a finger could be seen through it. Carved decor, so delicate that it only became visible when held to light, had also appeared. During the Ming copper red underglaze was added to the early blue-and-white underglaze, and colorful overglaze enamels also became popular. Reign marks, indicating the period during which the pieces were produced, also appeared on Ming porcelains from Jingdezhen and continued to be used through the early Qing.

The Qing Administration

In the late Ming a sub-prefect was permanently stationed at Jingdezhen to oversee the activities of the imperial factory. This position was continued in the early Qing, when a factory superintendent was sent by the court to oversee the imperial kilns. During the Qing, brilliant glazes like the eighteenth century "sang-de-boeuf" (oxblood) and the delicate "famille rose" enamels were added to the already enormous variety of porcelain decor. In addition, the Qing potters of Jingdezhen were superb craftsmen who could reproduce Song and Ming wares, often copying old pieces sent from the palace collections. In some cases, these copies are the only extant source of information about the original forms. The result of endless copying of previous styles, however, eventually led to a decline in the quality of the art. Also, working conditions, long difficult, now became increasingly bitter. During the reign of Qianlong the potter Zheng Zemou led his fellow workers to demand higher wages, and as a result conditions were improved. Later, however, Zheng was arrested and killed and his fellow potters were exiled to the frontier in chains. The small white aprons, which potters wear even today in Jingdezhen, are symbols of mourning for Zheng. In 1853 the city was destroyed during the turmoil of the Taiping Rebellion. A few of the kilns later

Opposite: Contemporary *mei-ping* vase, Jingdezhen

reopened, but by 1949 most had again been closed for years due to war and lack of markets.

Jingdezhen Today

After 1949 Jingdezhen relit fires in its kilns and the ailing enterprises were revived. The revitalized city was described as follows in 1955:

> The narrow streets of Chintehchen [Jingdezhen] are made narrower still by the rows of unfired pots that stand outside the houses drying in the sun. Down the middle of the streets, men push barrows loaded with clay, pinewood fuel for the kilns, or porcelain in various stages of completion. You have to step carefully here. Any unguarded movement might cause a breakage. . . . Go down any street, and you can watch the potters' wheels spinning as the clay takes on form beneath their practised fingers. Women sit busy with paintbrushes, their babies playing around their feet. Old grandmothers occupy themselves in putting the necessary 15 layers of glaze on the rice-pattern dinnersets – in which a design, resembling grains of rice, is stamped into the surface and the holes are filled with glaze so that they are translucent after firing. Smoke rises from the tall chimneys of the kilns and the markets are gay with colourful wares.[2]

Today Jingdezhen is once again the porcelain capital of China. The finest porcelains, pieces of extraordinary quality and artistic achievement, are created in the Fine Arts Porcelain Factory. The fine Jiangxi clays, second to none, are once again being shaped into tea sets, crockery, tableware, bowls, vases, and porcelain paintings, which are finished and painted by hand and require weeks or even months for completion. Underglaze painting is done in the old manner, on the unglazed, raw ware; costly "eggshell" bowls are still produced as modern treasures. Almost one thousand people work at the Fine Arts Porcelain Factory, and all of the work – enormously expensive – is for export. Another fine arts factory is devoted to small sculptures and turns out thousands of porcelain figurines each year. Other factories are fully automated for the mass production of porcelain dishes and household wares.

Jingdezhen is working to achieve the technological excellence of the West and has also established one of China's most advanced fine arts design and research institutes. Essentially a laboratory for advanced technology, the institute is also responsible for new designs, techniques, teaching, and overall planning for all the factories. It continues to research the past so as to preserve the history of this ancient art in modern reproductions.

[2]Mei Jianying, "City of Porcelain," *China Reconstructs,* February 1955, p. 14.

OTHER MODERN KILN CENTERS OF CHINA

In every region of China there are thousands of kilns in operation, producing the fine ceramic exports so important to modern China's economy. Some of these kilns have been in operation since the time of the Ming, or even earlier in a few cases. Each kiln is famous for a particular type of ware.

Shiwan, Foshan, Guangdong Province

The "pottery capital" of south China is Shiwan, whose pottery has been used for centuries for the everyday needs of the people of south China. Food is reputed to taste delicious when cooked in pots from Shiwan, and flower pots and storage jars with brilliant glazes decorate homes and parks. The kiln center, the largest in south China, is known for its fine crystalline glazes, professional artwork, everyday cookware, industrial porcelain, and small sculptures.

The Shiwan Fine Arts Studio produces beautiful glazed stoneware and pottery figurines, boldly modeled and colored with vivid glazes. Original designs for the small figures are produced by the studio's sculptors, and molds are made from these. The replicas are finished and glazed by hand with brilliant colors, then fired and polished with great care. The works, although mass-produced, receive attention from artisans with high professional standards. Traditional sculpture themes include historical and legendary figures, modern workers, fishermen, peasants, animals, and birds. The boldness of style has a vitality and simplicity that looks modern, and the facial features are emphasized by leaving flesh areas unglazed.

Modern figurine, Shiwan

Liling, Hunan Province

Traditional bird-and-flower paintings and scenes from the lush Hunan countryside decorate the bowls and vases of Liling. Design inspiration has also come from the ancient tomb objects found in 1971 in nearby Changsha, where several Han tombs were excavated. The varicolor underglaze, which has been achieved by extensive experimenting with pigments, is Liling's specialty. New colors have been developed here for underglaze painting. Mechanization is proceeding rapidly in the major industrial porcelain and mass-production factories in Liling, while the fine arts division remains one of the best in China. Liling is second only to Jingdezhen as a porcelain center.

Liling's ceramic factory

Modern Cizhou ware

Handan, Pengcheng, Hebei Province

Robust stonewares called Cizhou pottery were made here for the common people of north China, and today are produced again as art wares for the world. The decorative art of the Cizhou kilns went unappreciated by the Chinese elite of the Song period, who deemed it "suitable only for public eating places." But the rugged, free-spirited style must have been loved by millions of Chinese people, since they bought their everyday dishes and pots from the kilns in Cizhou or from one of the many other regional kilns which produced the same wares all over north China. A thousand years ago Pengcheng was given the name Cizhou, "pottery district," in recognition of its abundant pottery production.

Animals, insects, flowers, babies, good-luck patterns – all images which are loved by the people – decorate Cizhou ware. A small boy fishing was sketched on a white stoneware pillow one thousand years ago. Big peonies were created by carving through a black or brown glaze to the white slip, in a style called sgraffito. Such designs have the gay, often stylized, look of peasant embroidery. The florals were also sketched on the white slip in a quick, flowing freestyle using iron-rich pigments. The piece was then coated with a clear glaze and high-fired, a technique which anticipated the underglaze blue of Ming porcelain.

Yixing, Jiangsu Province

At Yixing serious tea drinkers choose the finest stoneware teapots. The unglazed stoneware teapots made of fine local clay are burnished after firing and decorated with designs of flowers, fruit, bamboo, or whole branches of plum blossoms modeled in relief.

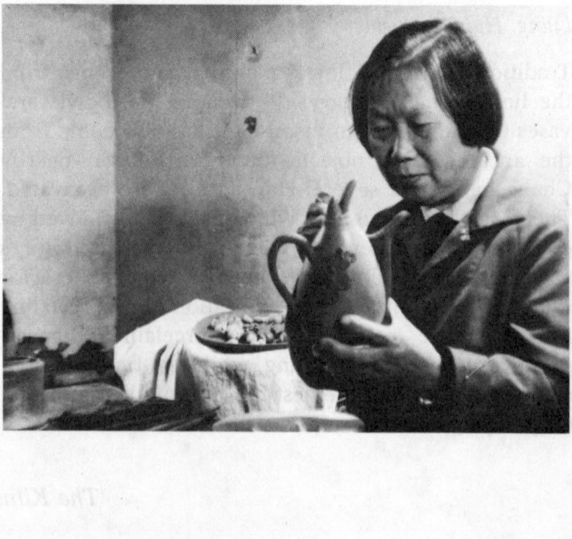

Veteran artist working on a Yixing teapot

Dehua, Fujian Province

Dehua is the historical center for "blanc de chine" statuettes of Buddha, Guan-yin, and other religious and legendary figures. The "blanc de chine" or "ivory" porcelain was formed into small sculptures, usually unadorned and pure white, molded and carved under a creamy, thick, translucent glaze. A major export center during the Ming and Qing, Dehua produced pieces found in museums throughout Europe. Figures were made in molds, and the same molds were often used for hundreds of years. Today artware and industrial porcelain are being produced.

Figurine from Dehua

Longquan, Southern Zhejiang Province

Longquan is another example of an ancient kiln, dormant for hundreds of years, which has come to life since the late 1950s. Fine celadons, a whole range of stoneware and porcelain covered with a thick, smooth, shiny glaze in shades of soft gray-green, with carved or relief decor under the glaze or a crackle glaze, are the specialty of these kilns.

Etching a traditional peony pattern on giant vases, Longquan Porcelain Factory

Jun, Yuxian, Henan Province

Latticed vase with two handles, Fengxi

A recently reopened kiln which in the past produced colored, glazed stonewares for the Song emperors, Jun is an example of the way in which ceramic research and archeology are revitalizing old kiln centers. Jun produces fine, solid stoneware with a thick glaze ranging from dove-gray to blue or red. Often several colors are mingled on the same piece.

Jun wares are among the finest of the ancient wares of the Song dynasty. Until the Song all the high-fired ceramic glazes were in tones of green; white and black had only recently been added. Probably as the result of an accident, red and purple streaks and mottles appeared on certain pieces fired at the Jun kilns. Fascinated, the potters experimented to discover the cause of these vivid effects, in order to reproduce the colors at will.

The soft tints of "moonwhite" and "blue of the sky after rain" were created from iron glazes, while red streaks and flambé effects were caused by spots of copper oxide in the glaze, producing different effects in varying kiln atmospheres. This was the beginning of the high-fired copper red glazes, which soon spread all over China to Jingdezhen, Shiwan, and Yixing, among other kilns. Over the next six centuries the "red glaze system" was perfected, culminating in the famous eighteenth century red glazes of Jingdezhen.

Fengxi, Shantou, Guangdong Province

The fine porcelains of Fengxi and Shantou are often decorated with elaborate pierced designs. Brilliantly enameled porcelains, often threaded with gold, are still made in southern kilns.

Tangshan, Hebei Province

Tangshan is a modern ceramic center which has expanded from a small kiln site to a planned factory complex. The center specializes in porcelain wares for export, but also has a fine art studio which creates large wall plaques, difficult to execute in porcelain.

Zibo, Shandong Province

Zibo is a very old kiln. For centuries a glass production center, Zibo today fashions fine ceramics with unusual and fanciful glazes like the "raindrop" glazes.

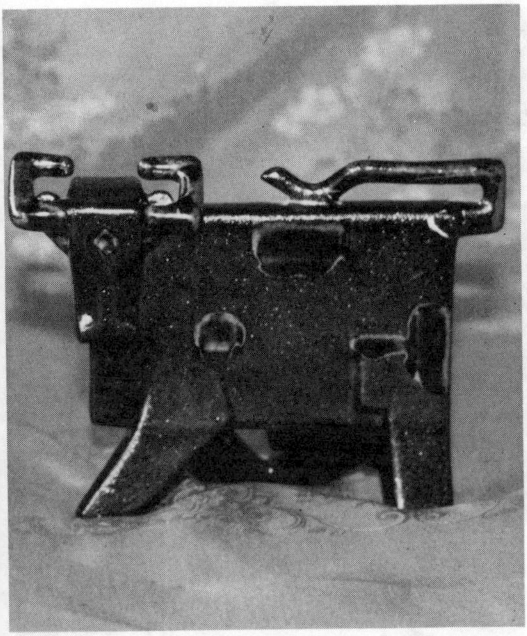

Above, left: Zibo cow. *Above:* Yaozhou ware

Yaozhou, Shaanxi Province

Yaozhou is one of the ancient kilns that resumed operations after centuries of disuse. It produced Northern Celadon, fine green wares with incised designs or impressed motifs made in pottery molds. In 1958 the first excavations were made at the site, and old pieces were collected, but it was not until 1974 that workers discovered the correct formulas. Today production has resumed on all the old varieties of pottery, along with new adaptations.

FOR FURTHER READING

Cosentino, Frank J. *The Boehm Journey to Ching-te-Chen, China, Birthplace of Porcelain.* Trenton, NJ: Edward Marshall Boehm, Inc., 1976.

Hobson, R.L. *Chinese Pottery and Porcelain.* New York: Dover, 1976.

Medley, Margaret. *The Chinese Potter.* Oxford: Phaidon, 1976.

Valenstein, S.G. *A Handbook of Chinese Ceramics.* New York: Metropolitan Museum of Art, 1975.

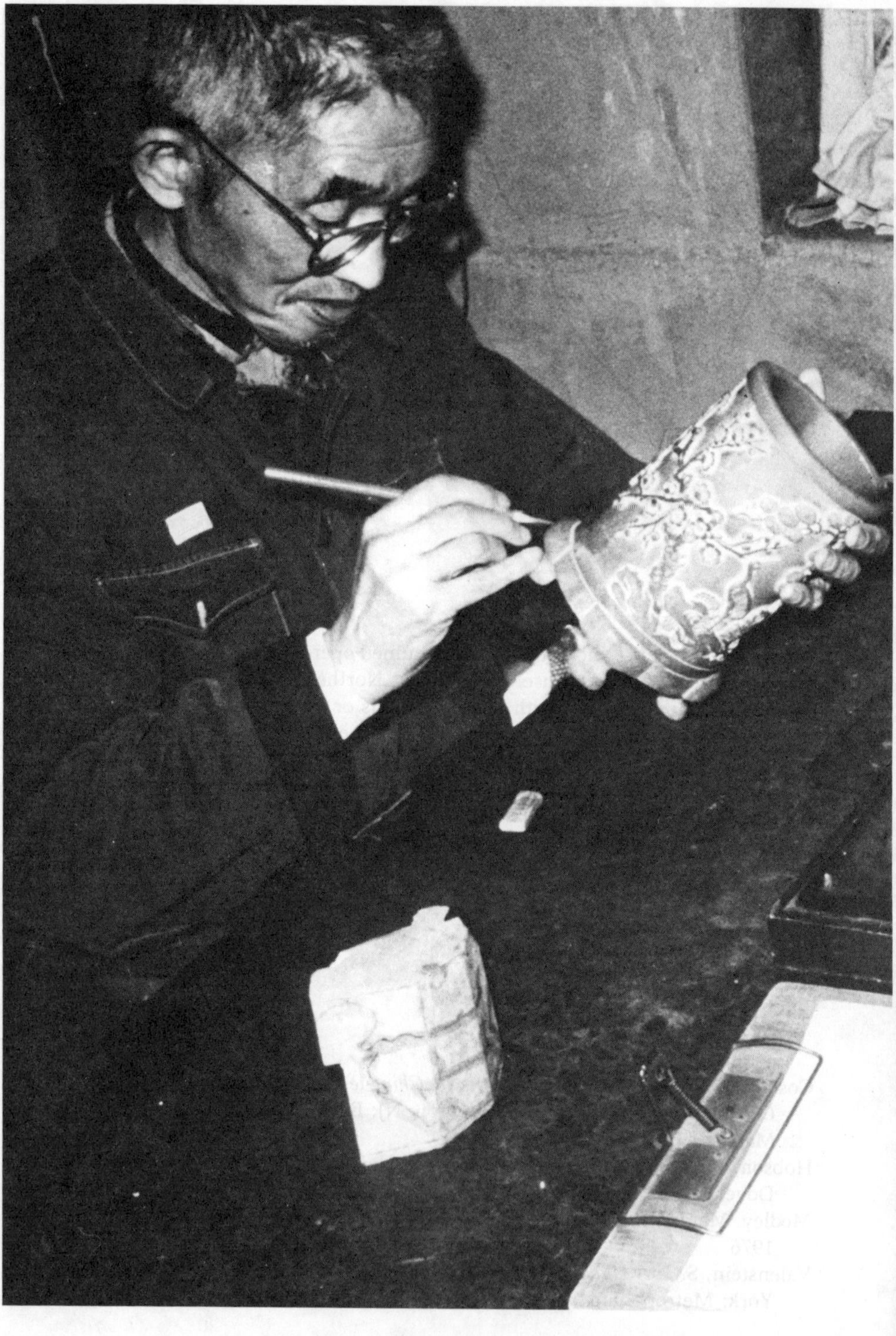

CHAPTER 5

JADE, HARDSTONES, AND IVORY

THE MAGICAL AURA OF JADE

Jade *bi,* Warring States period

To the ancient Chinese, jade was the most precious of stones, the symbol of all virtue, whose magical qualities made it more valuable than gold or silver. Jade was accorded immense value because of its physical properties – indestructibility, translucence, luster, resonance – which were associated with the human attributes of wisdom, purity, moral courage, power, and immortality. In the *Li Ji* classic, Confucius attributes these fine qualities to jade:

> Soft, smooth, and glossy, it appeared . . . like benevolence; fine, compact, and strong – like intelligence; angular, but not sharp and cutting – like righteousness; hanging down [in beads] as if it would fall to the ground – like [the humility of] propriety; when struck, yielding a note, clear and prolonged, yet terminating abruptly – like music; its flaws not concealing its beauty; nor its beauty concealing its flaws – like loyalty; with an internal radiance issuing from it on every side – like good faith; bright as a brilliant rainbow – like heaven; exquisite and mysterious, appearing in the hills and streams – like the earth; standing out conspicuously in the symbols of rank – like virtue; esteemed by all under the sky – like the path of truth and duty.[1]

Because the carved and polished stone was very beautiful, jade was admired for its beauty alone, while also valued for its other associations. *Yu*, the Chinese word for jade, acquired the additional meaning of purity and beauty, especially in describing lovely young women. The emperor carried jade scepters as emblems of authority, while nobles were given discs and other objects of jade as symbols of status and imperial favor.

Jade scabbard fitting, Han dynasty

The preeminent position of jade is reflected in the art and literature of China from its earliest history down through the centuries even to the present. An ancient legend tells the story of the lovely mortal, Chang E, who secretly drank the elixir of immortality and then

[1]James Legge, trans. *Li ki* [sic], Sacred Books of the East, vol. 4 (Oxford: Clarendon Press, 1885), p. 464.

flew to the moon. There in her palace she has a jade hare who prepares the wonderful potion in a cup with a jade pestle. During China's autumn festival, the people eat mooncakes and look up at the moon to see the lovely goddess, Chang E, in her palace.

Jade threads its way through all Chinese legends about the search for immortality. Ancient philosophers spoke of its pure and moral influences, while alchemists, fascinated by the stone's strength, tried to find ways to transmute its power. The consumption of jade was reputed to make one pure and indestructible, and ancient emperors drank a mix of powdered jade and water in an attempt to become immortal. Other recipes for eternal life called for spring waters flowing from the mountains where jade is found. Ancient books describe paradise as a mineral realm with trees and fruit of jade, and streams of flowing jade essence.

Jade burial suit, made of hundreds of pieces of jade sewn together with gold thread, Han dynasty

Jade deer, Zhou dynasty

Another legend described jade burial suits worn by nobles to guarantee their immortality. But when the tombs of the Han prince Liu Sheng and his wife were discovered in 1968, the legend became reality: over two thousand years ago the royal couple had been entombed in suits formed of thousands of squares of jade strung together with gold wire. Although the extravagant prince and his consort could afford to be completely covered with jade, the nobility were more often buried with selected jade ritual pieces around them.

The stone was just as important to the living, who wore charms and amulets of jade to ward off evil spirits or ensure good health. Lovely charms of entwined fish, often given to a bride, symbolized the joys of marriage and fidelity. Gifts of jade were also exchanged as tokens of friendship, and carved jade ornaments on a scholar's desk bespoke moral virtue and reverence for ancient ritual.

AS ENDURING AS CHINA: THE STORY OF JADE

In Neolithic times, before the technique of bronze casting was discovered in China, tools, weapons, axes, and knives were made of carved and polished stone. Tough and beautiful, nephrite, or jade, was the most highly prized mineral stone of this distant age, but nephrite objects are useless as tools owing to the brittle quality of the substance. Nephrite cannot be carved and is very difficult to grind, especially without metal tools. But modern experiments have demonstrated that this fibrous stone can indeed be ground with a tubular bamboo drill smeared with sand as an abrasive, although great patience and effort are required. The locations of the early sources of jade are uncertain, but there is no question about the rarity of the material and the difficulty in working it. Thus even at this early time jade knives and axes were perhaps reserved only for tribal chiefs. Nephrite was the hardest material known to the Neolithic people of China, and its symbolic association with indestructibility and purity had probably already begun.

Coiling jade dragon, Shang dynasty

Jade food vessel, Shang dynasty

When bronze weapons and tools replaced those of stone, the beautifully shaped and polished jade artifacts found in the tombs of the time retained only ritual significance. The use of metal-tipped bamboo drills enabled the jade carver to use more freedom in creation. Flat slabs of jade about half an inch thick were carved into knives, axes, and various shapes, such as circles, semicircles, and animals incised with geometric patterns. Certain jade symbols recur in this ceremonial age.

CEREMONIAL JADE

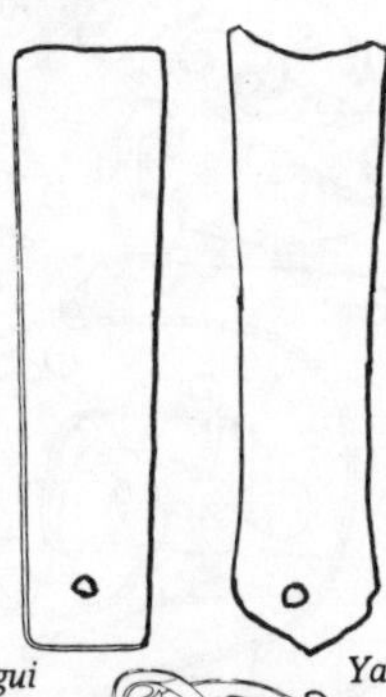

Zhen-gui *Yan-gui*

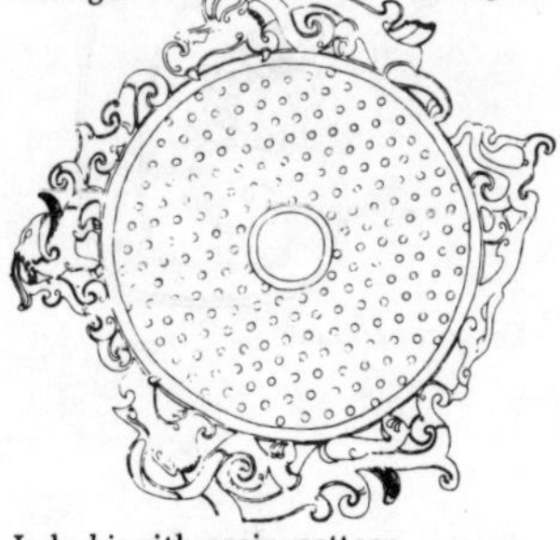

Jade *bi* with grain pattern

The *zhen-gui*, a flat, oblong sheet with a single hole, probably derives from the Stone Age axe. An important token of authority and symbol of power, the *zhen-gui* was carried by the king on ceremonial occasions. Each court rank was assigned its own scepter-like jade shape.

The *yan-gui* was carried by official envoys as a token of royal authority.

The flat *bi* is a disc with a central hole. By the time of the Shang, the *bi* was carried by lower ranking nobility, although it retained a special religious significance. It was the symbol of heaven, used in ceremonies by the emperors of China until the last dynasty.

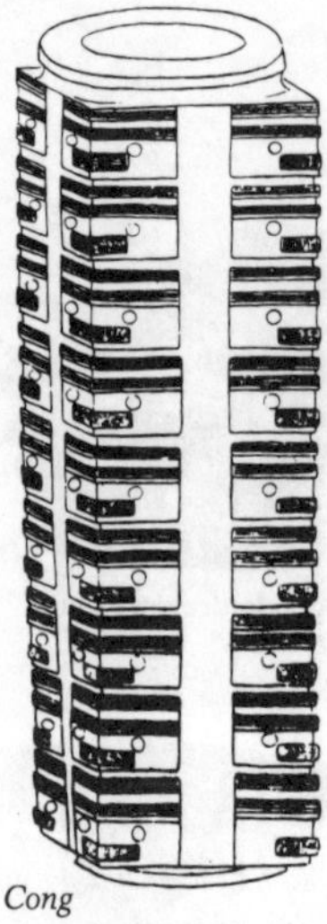

Cong

The *cong* was a cylinder within a square tube, symbolizing the earth.

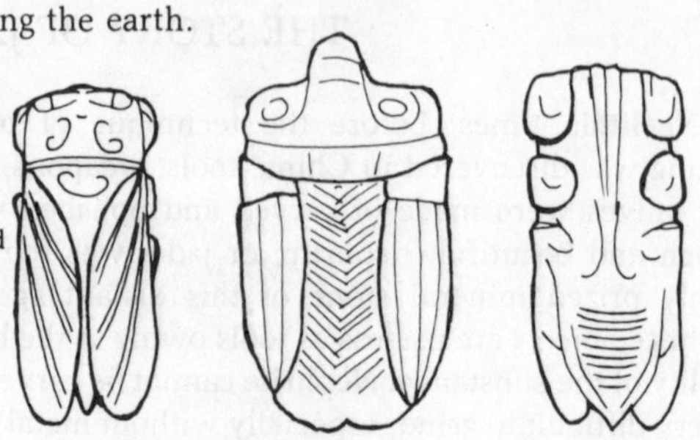

Cicada-shaped amulets

The elaborate burial rituals of the Zhou also incorporated many of these symbolic ornaments. Jade *bi* were placed on and around the corpse in a strictly prescribed manner; jade was placed in body orifices, and a jade cicada on the tongue. The cicada, since it sheds its old skin to emerge anew, probably symbolized resurrection. Jade ornaments such as pendants and hairpins were also used during the Shang and Zhou, though purely for decoration.

AMULETS AND LOVE TOKENS

By the late Zhou and Han, not only the nobility but also rich merchants and the rising landowning class had begun to acquire expensive jade ornaments and amulets. Designs grew freer and bolder. Belt hooks, clasps, earrings, and hairpins of jade – even the *bi* disc – became exquisite ornaments designed solely for pleasure. Jade pendants, which hung from the girdle and made a pleasant tinkling sound, were fashioned as charming miniatures. Jade objects were also worn as

Dragon pendant

Animal knocker, Han dynasty

charms and amulets, as beautiful decorations, or given as tokens of friendship and love.

Iron drills and cutting discs facilitated the carving of vases, cups, and other larger shapes. With the rise of a class of scholars, a small elite group of men who could read and write, jade was increasingly used to make desk implements and seals.

JADE AND THE IMAGES OF BUDDHISM

Buddhism brought to China the symbols and sculptural styles of India; Buddhist statues, monumental and miniature, began to appear in caves and temples throughout China from the fourth century on. During Buddhism's hundreds of years as a prominent religion in China, itinerant Chinese artisans and urban craftsmen used their traditional techniques to transform the images of India into uniquely Chinese symbols. Even today Chinese artists continue to create exquisitely carved ivory and jade statues of Buddhas, guardian figures, and Guan-yin, the Goddess of Mercy. Buddhist symbols include "Buddha's hand" citron and bowls in the shape of lotus flowers. In this way, Buddhism has added to the repertoire of symbols used through the centuries in all Chinese crafts. Craftsmen also perfected the technique of using the natural colors of raw jade to enhance the final object.

THE EMPEROR WHO LOVED JADE

In 1680 under the Qing emperor Kang-xi, imperial crafts workshops were established in Beijing, and the country's finest jade craftsmen were brought there to work. Jade was now shaped into elaborate pieces such as vases, incense burners, and covered bowls. The eighteenth-century Qing emperor, Qian-long, had a passion for jade. He had samples of his poetry inscribed on selected objects of fine jade. Imperial seals were beautifully carved in ivory and jade to suit the exacting taste of the emperor. The finest jade was brought from Xinjiang for the exclusive use of the imperial workshops (although much of this was secretly diverted for sale to private shops). Artists in the palace workshops were given great freedom and all the time necessary to create elaborate works with the finest materials that money could buy.

It was also at this time that jade was used for such implements as the brush pot, brush rest, signature seal, table screen, incense container, and finely carved animals. Jade screens kept the breeze from riffling the papers on the scholar's desk, but they also had a more subtle use. Often these screens were carved with landscapes, especially in the centuries after the rise of land-

Jade weight with hare decoration, Tang dynasty

Detail of "Yu Taming the Waters," Qing dynasty

scape painting. Carved in low relief, their miniature mountains and valleys were peopled with wise old hermits, immortal beings, and marvelous animals. Simply by raising his eyes to the screen, the scholar could be transported to this wonderful realm and find inspiration for his poetry or painting. At the same time wafting clouds of incense would emerge from a censer in the shape of a mountain, complete with miniature people and animals. These hill censers, often of jade, were important in creating the proper mood for artistic creation.

Much of the work of this time was distinguished by its freshness, vitality, and originality. Cameo techniques made skillful use of the streaks of color in the jade, with one color being carved in relief to stand out from the background. Elaborate openwork and fanciful high reliefs also became more prevalent, as styles became increasingly rococco. Large pieces of jade were fashioned, including one massive example called "Yu Taming the Waters," now on display at the Palace Museum. It was executed by carvers in Yangzhou, Jiangsu Province; weighing more than five and a half tons, the final sculpture took several carvers many years to complete. Private guilds also flourished, supported by foreign trade, and craft shops lined the streets of major cities throughout the nineteenth and early twentieth centuries.

THE WAR YEARS

Skilled craftsmen needed materials and commissions to survive, and the growing political and economic instability of the early twentieth century destroyed the demand for luxury wares. Artisans were reduced to making trinkets and amulets of jade or ivory chopsticks and mahjong pieces for foreign buyers. The only other available work came from dealers and middlemen who provided materials but paid only a pittance for the finished commission – often stale, unimaginative copies of an earlier piece. According to Pang Binghen, one of the first directors of the Beijing Arts and Crafts Research Institute, by 1950 there were only about one hundred jade carvers left in Beijing. A carver himself, Pang found his situation desperate as the Sino-Japanese War disrupted sales of jade. He and other master carvers were forced to become servants or pedicab drivers in order to survive. The artists were determined, however, to continue practicing on wood and stone whenever possible, so that they would not lose their hard-earned skills, acquired by long apprenticeship working sixteen-hour days with next to nothing in payment.

Teapot in ancient style

JADE CARVING TODAY

A MODERN JADE WORKSHOP

In 1953 the carvers formed cooperatives so they could obtain the fine precious and semiprecious stones they needed for their work and sell their crafts without recourse to exploitative dealers. The Beijing Arts and Crafts Research Institute purchased research materials for their use, including art works and manuals from previous dynasties; they also began transcribing records of the experience and knowledge of veteran craftsmen. Artists were encouraged to enlarge their knowledge and adopt new themes, using figures from Chinese classics, history, legends, and mythology.

In 1958 all the carvers' cooperatives were incorporated into the present Beijing Jade Studios. Today more than fourteen hundred carvers work in a modern four-story building, and hundreds of boys and girls are student apprentices. The first technological innovation in jade-carving technique came when the old treadle-driven lathes which turned the cutting disc were replaced with electric lathes. This permitted artisans to devote their attention to the design and grinding process, instead of exhausting themselves in driving the lathes with foot power. In addition to training the new generation, the studios have helped to establish jade workshops in other cities. At present there are more than one hundred jade studios in China with over twenty thousand carvers. Beijing is still the largest center and today produces some of the most beautiful jade sculpture since the eighteenth century, with the most varied and imaginative motifs.

A legendary *qilin*

TRAINING A NEW GENERATION OF ARTISANS

Training apprentices is an important function of the older crafts masters. After graduation from middle school, young people interested in becoming jade carvers must take an aptitude test. They must also be dedicated, as the craft will take many years to master. The young jade carver first becomes familiar with carving one type of object. Producing a jade bowl and lid roughly based on an old design, for example, will probably take about a year. When the apprentice carver finishes the piece, he or she will make another one much like the first. The carver will often use a reproduction of an old museum piece as a model or source of inspiration. Sometimes, as is frequent in Chinese craft history, the model is of a different material from the copy; thus a jade bowl may be based upon a bronze model.

Polishing a jade bowl

Children of jade carvers and other craft workers still tend to follow in the footsteps of their fathers, but with one enormous difference. Large numbers of women have today chosen this craft; a totally inconceivable notion in the old society, the participation of women is today considered the norm.

JADE AND HARDSTONE CARVING: TECHNIQUES AND MATERIALS

Many thousands of years of carving experience have given the Chinese sculptor complete mastery of the techniques of carving. Before the chisel or drill is even lifted, the artist must carefully consider the raw stone or block, noting its special qualities, inner patterns, and grain. A design and subject must be selected appropriate to these characteristics. The process, almost mystical at times, requires a great familiarity and experience with the varieties, structures, and patterns of gemstones. The best sculpture incorporates the natural patterns of the raw material, such as streaks of color in mineral stones, as an integral part of the final design. Bringing out the unique qualities and hidden beauty of natural materials is one of the special skills of the Chinese carver.

HARDSTONES

Although jade is considered by the Chinese to be the most precious of all stones, many other precious and semiprecious hardstones were carved and continue to be carved today in jade workshops. These include agate, coral, rose and black quartz, sapphire, turquoise, malachite, and rock crystal, to name a few. Traditionally, jasper, amethyst, serpentine, lapis lazuli, and aven-

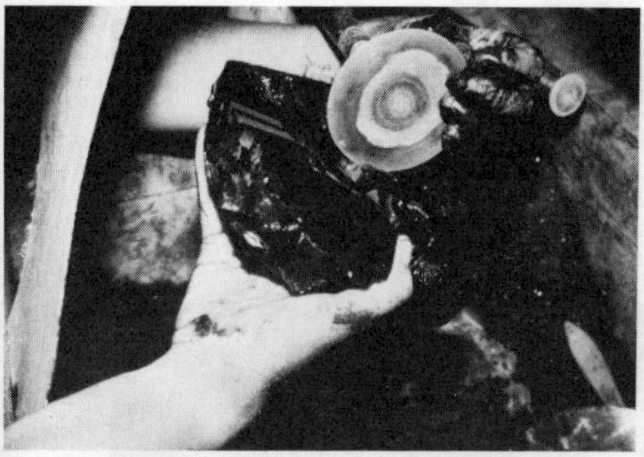

Above, left: Grinding jade with an abrasive paste. *Above, right:* Rough-cutting with a rotary blade

turine (quartz) were highly valued for small sculpture, inlay, or jewelry.

The tools of the carver vary little from one material to another. Knives of various shapes, cutting discs, drills, chisels, gougers, and polishers are all used; the nature of the material determines the strength or fineness of the cutting tool. Work on jade and other hardstones requires the use of an abrasive harder than the material to be carved.

WHAT IS JADE?

Formerly the Chinese term *yu* indicated a number of hard, rare, or beautiful stones, including agate and quartz, but nephrite alone was held to be "true jade" (*zhen-yu*) and has been prized since Neolithic times in China. Another closely related mineral, jadeite, has also been included in the category of jade, but was introduced much later, probably in the eighteenth century.

Nephrite

Nephrite is a heavy mineral stone which rates 6 to 6.5 on the 10-point Mohs scale for hardness. The mineral is not as hard as a number of other substances, yet its particular structure, formed in the earth under great pressure, results in fibrous rock of great hardness. Nephrite is found in the mountains of Xinjiang Province, and it has been exported from there for centuries. Nephrite boulders and pebbles are found in river beds, as well as in rock formations worked in mines and quarries. When polished, nephrite has an oily luster. The stone is cold to the touch, resonant, and translucent when thinly cut. The modern Chinese term for nephrite is *ruan-yu*, or "soft jade."

Jadeite

Jadeite is a granular mineral even tougher than nephrite, but equally heavy. Like nephrite, jadeite is formed in the earth under high pressure. The two

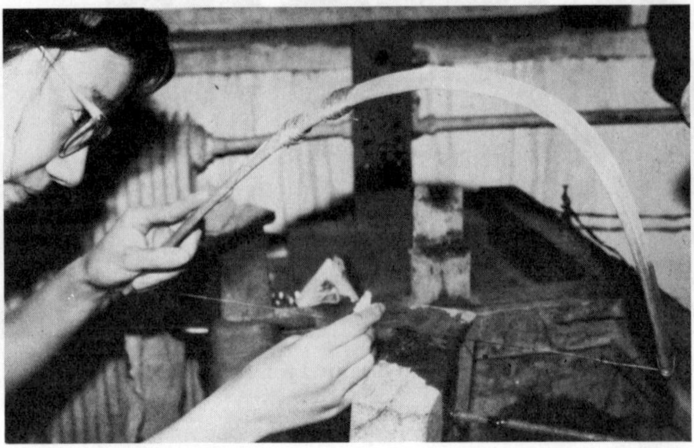
Using a bamboo saw

stones are difficult to differentiate. Despite their hardness, both stones crack easily—jadeite more easily than nephrite. Polished jadeite has a brilliant, glasslike finish. The modern Chinese term for jadeite is *ying-yu*, or "hard jade."

Colors

Jadeite and nephrite occur in a broad range of colors from white, yellow, and red to indigo blue, gray, and black, as well as the best known varieties, the green tones. The most precious types of both jadeite and nephrite are pure white in color. Called "muttonfat" jade, they were compared to the rich, translucent, and unctuous texture of congealed lard. Often veins and flecks of several colors appear on one boulder, due to the presence of iron, manganese, chromium, and other elements. The muttonfat variety with vermilion flecks is highly prized, as are stones of spinach green splashed with gold, the so-called moss amid melting snow, which contain veins of green amid pale white, and the emerald "kingfisher" jadeite.

THE CARVING OF JADE

Because of its tough composition, jade cannot be cut or carved, strictly speaking, but is ground by the use of an abrasive powder of an even harder material. Quartz crystals, crushed garnets, or rubies were used before the discovery of the synthetic carborundum, which is widely used today in China. The grinding effect is due to the slow action of the abrasive paste, rather than to the action of the cutting tools.

The abrasive paste is used with a small electric rotary disc, called a lap wheel, or with a steel drill. Large pieces of jade are first rough-cut with a wire saw and abrasive paste. Then various discs and gougers of graduated size aid the artist in shaping the progressively finer lines in the work. Pieces to be hollowed are pierced and bored out with a diamond drill. By these methods a carver with great experience and infinite patience creates intricate and delicate objects such as a chain of separately moveable but interlocking links cut from a single piece of jade. The final step is polishing by the use of polishers and leather buffers with an abrasive paste. This painstaking process produces the fluent lines and silken softness of the final object, whose pliant molding belies the labor in its manufacture.

CREATING DESIGNS

The artist working in jade and hardstones must be extremely skillful, painstaking, careful, and patient; completion of a work may take anywhere from several months to several years. A design is never created before the jade or hardstone is carefully studied, and every streak or spot of color, every aspect of grain and texture thoroughly examined. Flaws or imperfections may become a part of the design or may be cleverly cut away. The design is finally the product of the carver's creative vision, or sometimes the collaboration of carver and designer or master and apprentice. Such artists must have a creative imagination which allows them to "see" within the stone and "release" the bird, fish, or animal captured there. Carving is the art of subtraction, never of addition. Skilled carvers must be able to determine in advance which way a vein of color will travel; during the grinding process they must listen to the sounds of the stone to judge the progress of the sculpture. Thus, for example, a jade plaque of pale green goldfish carved in high relief incorporates a vein of red as one of the fish. A gray agate horse uses a streak of pink as the mane and saddle. Black flecks in a piece of turquoise are made to appear as a design on a fan held by a famous figure from Chinese literature.

Adding the final details

IVORY

Although ivory never held the same importance as jade, it too was a rare imported material always in great demand among nobles, scholars, and rich merchants as a symbol of status. Derived from elephant tusks, the teeth and horns of whale, walrus, hippopotamus, rhinoceros, and boar, ivory may occur in a variety of tones from purest white to yellow and even brown. The material is valued by carvers for its grain, smooth texture, and rich, natural feel. Ivory can be polished to a high sheen, and fine old pieces have often acquired a special gloss from long handling. It absorbs moisture readily and will crack if exposed to extremes of moisture, dryness, or temperature. A relatively soft material, ivory requires no abrasive for sculpting.

IVORY IN ANCIENT TIMES

In carving ivory, as in other crafts, there was an interweaving of motifs, and whatever was carved in one material invariably was carved in others. The Chinese sculptor was unique in his ability to create art objects in almost any available material. The Shang craftsman fashioned sculpture of bone and ivory, often incorporating the same flat, linear, and zoomorphic style of decoration seen on early bronze. Elephants, which existed in northern China in prehistoric times, were still found there until about the middle of the first millennium BC, and their tusks provided ivory for ornamental objects and vessels inlaid with turquoise stones.

TWO SCHOOLS OF CARVING

Ivory carving may be separated into two schools, the northern and the southern. The northern style, exemplified by the ivories produced in Beijing during the Ming and Qing dynasties, is characterized by creative and meticulous craftsmanship. Landscapes and figures are combined in sculptures which incorporate realism with imaginative and decorative elements. The style is also characterized by use of traditional techniques such as openwork and rhythmic interweaving of elements.

The southern style of ivory carving, centered in Guangzhou, is more elaborate and may feature subjects such as the traditional ornate flower boats and the famous multiple concentric balls. During most of the Qing dynasty, Guangzhou was the center of trade between China and the rest of the world. Generation after

Carving an ivory tusk

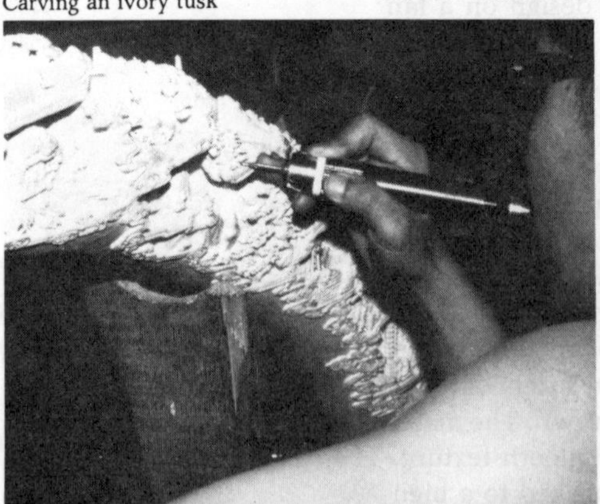

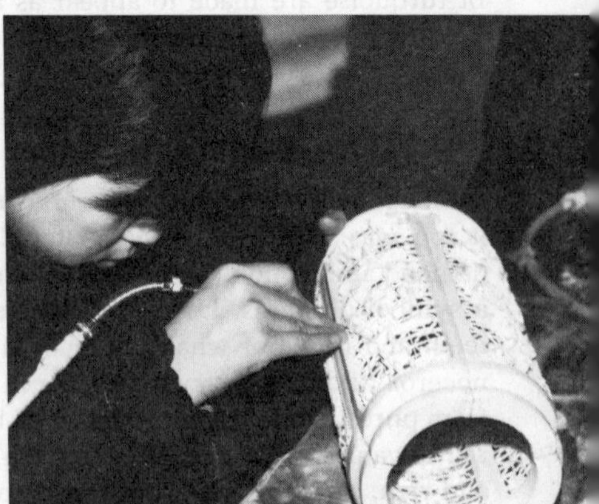

Above, left: Carving an ivory figurine. *Above, right:* Working on concentric spheres

generation of ivory and jade carvers worked here, and painting and enameling thrived because of the strong demand for art. In the seventeenth century Guangzhou ivory carvers were so renowned for their superior skill that they were summoned to Beijing by the Kang-xi emperor to work in the palace workshops he had established. These workshops produced amazingly detailed and elaborate landscapes of ivory, often complete with human and animal figures and added designs in filigree. Carved ivory was also used as inlay in fine wood and lacquer furniture.

Carving concentric balls, each of which spins freely within the others, has been a special skill of Guangzhou carvers for centuries and is today a specialty of the modern Daxin (Guangzhou) ivory carvers. More than forty of these concentric spheres have been carved from a single ivory globe. The carving process involves drilling diagonal holes to permit the use of a special right-angled tool to carve the spheres, working from the inside to the outside. The artisan can tell if the tool is accurately positioned only by its sound and feel. The last step is to carve the surface of each sphere, working back from the outside to the inside, adding intricate filigree designs at each stage. Often the spinning balls are part of a total design, as in the stunning modern sculpture of the moon goddess Chang E, who is pictured flying from the Moon, sphere within sphere, down to earth.

FOR FURTHER READING

Hansford, S.H. *Jade: Essence of Hills and Streams.* New York: American Elsevier, 1969.

Hartman, J. *Chinese Jade of Five Centuries.* Rutland, VT: C.E. Tuttle, 1969.

Painstaking silk embroidery at the world-renowned Suzhou Embroidery Research Institute

CHAPTER 6

SILK WEAVING AND EMBROIDERY

For dancing girls of Chaoyang, [a] token of
profoundest favor,
One set of spring robes worth a thousand
in gold–
To be stained in sweat, rouge-soiled, never worn
again,
Dragged on the ground, trampled in mud–who
is there to care?
The *liao-ling* weave takes time and toil,
Not to be compared to common *tseng* or *po*;
Thin threads endlessly plied, till the
weaver's fingers ache;
Clack-clack the loom cries a thousand
times but less than a foot is done.
You singers and dancers of the Chaoyang Palace,
Could you see her weaving, you'd pity her too!

"LIAO-LING SILK"
Bai Juyi (Tang dynasty)[1]

WOMEN'S WORK

Raising silkworms, silk weaving, and embroidery were primarily arts of the women of China. In Chinese folklore Lei-zu, wife of the legendary Yellow Emperor, discovered the secret of silk and passed it on to Chinese women. Sitting in her garden, she heard the sound of rustling leaves overhead and saw silkworms spinning their cocoons with silken thread. "How wonderful," she thought, "if this soft thread could be woven into cloth!" This was the beginning of sericulture, one of China's unique contributions to the world.

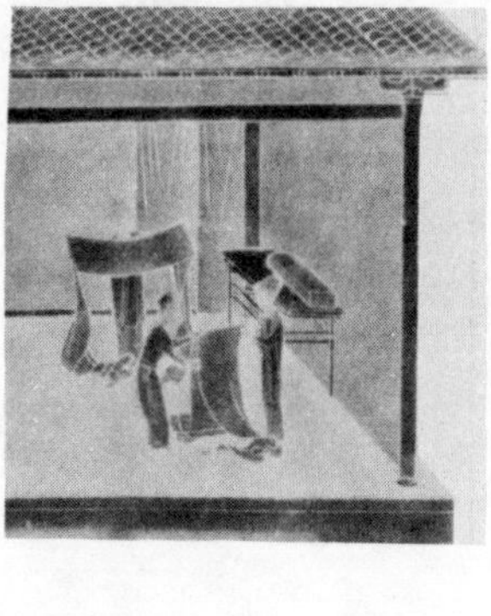

In old China it was mainly women's work to raise silkworms, reel thread, weave cloth, and create embroideries called "paintings in thread." The festival on the seventh day of the seventh lunar month celebrating the meeting in heaven of the Weaving Maid and the Herd Boy symbolized the duty of men to farm and women to sew. The heavenly lovers are the stars Vega and Altair; according to legend, they are kept apart all year so that he will tend his ox and she will weave at her loom

[1]Burton Watson, *Chinese Lyricism* (New York: Columbia University Press, 1971), p. 186.

undistracted. Their annual meeting became a festival day especially celebrated by women, a time to pray for the most important attributes a woman could have – beauty and skill with a needle.

Women in old China had a very lowly position. When a girl was married, usually to a man she had never seen, she left her home and became a part of her husband's family. Not infrequently, the young bride had a very hard life serving her new family. A young woman who brought to her new home great skill in weaving and embroidery had a chance to improve her lot and gain higher status. In poor families a skilled embroiderer could work at home on jobs farmed out by private and imperial workshops. During the Tang dynasty, women were required to weave silk or linen as part of a "cloth" tax levied by the emperor. Rich families gave the work to servant girls. Little wonder a woman prayed to the heavenly Weaving Maid. She prayed for fine embroidery needles and silken thread; she prayed for a miracle which would make her skillful with the needle.

Skill in needlework was passed down the generations from mother to daughter. Training started very young, and, later, when women married, embroidery often became the one creative and artistic outlet encouraged by society.

Needlework probably arose with the discovery of silk. From earliest times needlework has been an important folk craft, and gaily embroidered clothes and banners were a necessary part of weddings and festivals. By the Ming dynasty, silk was plentiful and relatively cheap; the homes of nobles, scholars, and wealthy urban merchants were covered with embroidered household items–wall hangings, bedspreads, tablecloths, and paneled folding screens. Fine textiles were essential to these homes. Shimmering brocades and damasks were sometimes handwoven for dining room chairs and cushions. Children's clothing and women's skirts, jackets, parasols, shawls, slippers, and purses were woven and embroidered at home. Wives and daughters of court officials sometimes embroidered the mandarin squares, emblems of status worn on the robes of civil servants and their wives.

Like her urban sister, the cotton-clad village woman learned to embroider early in life. Cotton for clothing appeared late in China's history; up until the tenth century, common people wore clothes of woven hemp or other plant fibers such as flax. Embroidery pattern books became part of a young woman's inheritance, handed down from generation to generation. The folk art of papercutting is directly related to peasant embroidery patterns, and both of these arts reached great heights in Zhejiang and Jiangsu provinces in central China, where silk was produced in abundance. In fact, many farm women and their families in these provinces worked on the whole range of silk processes; they raised the silkworms, boiled the cocoons, reeled the thread, wove the cloth, and finally embroidered small pieces of cloth for sale.

THE SECRET OF SILK

The true beginnings of silk culture and weaving are lost in prehistory, but at least four thousand years ago the secret of silk was already well known in China. Many written characters used in silk culture have been found scratched on Shang dynasty oxbones from the second millennium BC, and artifacts show that rulers and nobles of the Bronze Age wore garments of variegated silk.

In early centuries a good "harvest" of silk became almost as important as a good grain harvest. Chinese emperors participated in a series of sacred rites at the beginning of the planting season, imploring the help of heaven during the following year. Parallel rites were performed by the empress, who began the yearly cultivation of silkworms with ceremonies which included gathering mulberry leaves from the palace trees for feed and praying for a fine year's production of silken thread. Vast quantities of silk were collected in taxes. Emperors gave bolts of silk as gifts to foreign emissaries and as tokens of favor to faithful generals and ministers. Silk even became a medium of exchange, like gold in the West.

ROBES AND RANK

The ancient rulers and their courts were the elite of Chinese society. Their robes were not only decoration in keeping with their fine palaces and luxurious surroundings; they were also displays of official rank, symbolically expressing their duties and privileges. Official costumes were an important part of rigid ceremonial protocol. In fact, Han law required that special silk gowns with the appropriate insignia be kept by all court officials for ceremonial occasions. Soft, beautifully designed, and richly embroidered, these silken robes stimulated the development of the textile arts. Silk used the conventions, symbols, and motifs which became an essential part of the language of Chinese art, the design repertoire that was handed down from one dynasty to the next. Embroidery was one of the first graphic arts in China, preceding the development of painting.

The needs of the ancient courts for costumes and decorative fabrics were enormous. By the Han, silk weaving and embroidery had become a highly organized craft industry, with two imperial weaving workshops in the capital and numerous other workshops in the provinces; thousands of skilled craftsmen were employed in these workshops. The recently excavated tomb of a Han noblewoman, wife of the Marquis Dai, reveals the extent and importance of the silk industry. Roll after roll of well-preserved silk satins, figured brocades, and gauzes as thin as modern nylon were found, as well as an extensive wardrobe of embroidered silk robes and many yards of embroidered damask for the noblewoman's use in the next world. The vast imperial requirements for silk continued through all the dynasties. The opulent style of court life in the Tang is exemplified by one imperial concubine, Yang Guifei, who required seven hundred artisans to weave her silk robes.

THE ROMANCE OF THE SILK ROAD

By about the middle of the Zhou dynasty (ca. 1066–256 BC), China had already begun to export silk to the Middle East across an old caravan trail which later became known as the Silk Road. Silk quickly became the principle medium of trade between China and the rest of the world. The Silk Road crossed the vast deserts from the Han capital of Changan (present-day Xian) to Syria on the Mediterranean, seven thousand kilometers away. The trip was immensely dangerous; caravans had to cross treacherous mountain passes and desert wastes and pass through the territories of hostile

"The Silk Road," reproduction of Tang polychrome

nomadic tribes. Traders could only get across the western deserts with the Bactrian camel, which could smell water in the sand and was reputed to give warning of coming sandstorms. Small painted clay camels loaded with bolts of silk have been found in Tang tombs and provide a glimpse of these desert caravans. From the fourth to the tenth century, in caves along the Silk Road devout Buddhists built temples with awesome sculptures and murals that are preserved even today by the dry desert air. Pieces of fabric have also been found perfectly preserved in the sand.

To the ancient Greeks, China was known as the mysterious land of silk at the edge of the world. Several centuries later, robes of gauzy, luxurious woven silk were much in demand among Roman senators and noblewomen, who called China the land of the "Seres" or silk people. The mania for thin, shimmering, brilliantly colored silks was a continual source of support for Chinese textile crafts. Indeed, silk kept the Han emperors rich and powerful, since the West was willing to pay a pound of gold for a pound of raw silk.

Silk production was a jealously guarded Chinese secret. The Romans thought that silk was a type of vegetable fiber, and as long as China alone could provide this gossamer fabric, a thriving trade with the Middle East was assured. Taking silkworms out of the country was punishable by death; not until about the middle of the sixth century was the secret of silk production finally smuggled to the West. According to one legend, a Chinese princess going to Khotan to be married hid the precious silkworm eggs in her headdress. In another tale, two Persian monks hid the eggs in hollow walking sticks and spirited them to Byzantium. By this time silk weaving and embroidery had become highly advanced arts relying upon an extensive and sophisticated industry. Textiles were considered a major art form, not merely a decorative art as in the West.

Trade along the Silk Road eventually brought to the Persians and Europeans not only silk but the drawlooms needed to weave intricate damask and brocade textiles. The designs of the silks sent to the West included animals and flowers, hunting scenes, and geometric figures – all the lively patterns of Han art. To China came a whole new repertoire of designs – the now familiar rosettes and medallions with stylized birds facing each other in rigid symmetry. In fact, the Silk Road became a channel for new influences which enriched all Chinese crafts.

During the Tang dynasty, fourteen hundred years ago, the Silk Road was bustling with trading caravans whose journey terminated at the great metropolis of Changan; overland commerce in silk reached its peak at this time.

DRAGON ROBES: SYMBOLS OF POWER

Silk was the foundation for the magnificent dragon robes worn by the emperor and his officials. A complex symbolism of rank had developed over the centuries of imperial rule, and the ceremonial robes were the means of its expression. The emperor was the center of the universe – indeed, he *was* the universe when he wore his robes strewn with cosmic symbols. The officials who stood before him at court were clearly ranked in turn by the emblems on their dragon robes. By the Ming, the dragon robes had become the embodiment of the whole Chinese feudal and imperial system.

All of the dragon robes incorporated symbols of prosperity, longevity, and good fortune, as their name indicates. All of the robes contained dragon designs embroidered into the silk. The dragon robes worn by the emperor, however, were exclusive in several respects. The large, coiling, five-clawed dragons on the center front and back of the emperor's robe were the emperor's personal symbol. (The dragon symbol had been associated with imperial power as far back as the Shang dynasty.) The emperor alone could wear the twelve symbols of authority, which had first been used in very ancient times on robes worn by the ruler for sacrifical rites. The twelve symbols included the sun, moon, and stars, representing heaven; the mountain, representing earth; the dragon and pheasant, representing creatures of sea and air; sacrificial goblets, representing respect for the ancestors; water weed, representing purity; grain, representing care for the people; fire, represent-

Detail of emperor's robe, facing page

Emperor's robe with the twelve symbols of authority, Qing dynasty

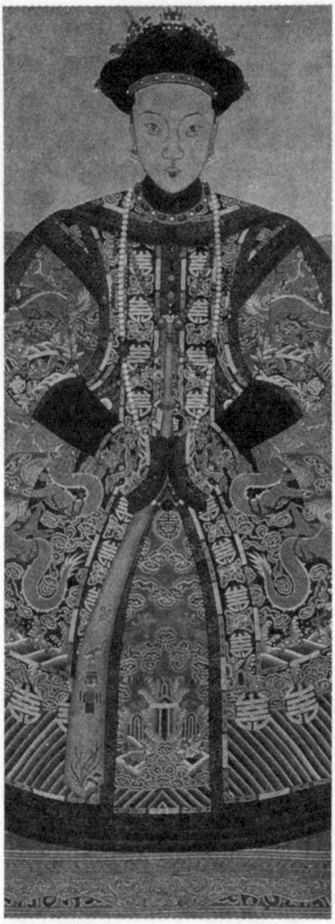

ing brilliance; and the ax and Fu symbol. The last two symbolized the emperor's exclusive power of punishment and judgment.

The robes worn by officials at court, and by their wives, incorporated some of the twelve symbols of authority, but never all twelve. Mandarin squares–emblems of rank–were worn on the front and back of outer robes of officials and their wives. These panels were separate pieces, so they could be changed as rank changed; birds or animals, and sometimes mythological creatures, were embroidered on these magnificent squares to denote rank. Civil officials wore emblems with birds, such as cranes or pheasants, while military officials wore animals, such as lions or *qilin* (unicorns).

The dragon robes were woven in imperial workshops on especially large drawlooms. The background of satin or figured silk furnished a rich foundation for embroidery, and designers also used plain weaves of silk or light-weight gauze for summer robes. Dyes had to be absolutely accurate, since specific colors indicated rank and category of position. The emperor's official robes were bright yellow, although he might wear other colors. Royal princes wore red robes with dragon medallions. Writhing dragons were embroidered with gleaming satin stitches, flat and even, couched in gold thread, while tiny seed stitches punctuated floral designs. A single robe could easily take four to five years to complete. Master artists used all of their skill in design and their full appreciation of the artistic potential of silk to create true masterpieces of embroidery.

TAPESTRY: PAINTINGS WOVEN IN SILK

Thousand of looms in the lower Yangzi Valley were already producing woven silk commercially over fourteen hundred years ago. The steadily growing weaving industry reached its height about a thousand years ago, when techniques were developed which used a greater density of threads per inch, and finer spun silk yarns. *Ke-si*, or "cut silk," tapestries had so many tightly packed warp and weft threads that they were used to create paintings in silk. This exquisite weaving was used to mount fine paintings, to make covers for the Buddhist sutras, and especially to create panels for screens and wall hangings. *Ke-si* mandarin squares woven with symbols of rank and elaborate and beautiful tapestry collars were also made for the robes of the emperor and court officials.

Mandarin square of brocaded satin with *qilin* design, Ming dynasty

During the Ming dynasty *ke-si* panels were exported to Europe, where they were incorporated into the vestments used in European cathedrals. From the time of the Ming to the nineteenth century, endless rolls of Chinese figured silks were exported to the West. Chinoiserie – Chinese-inspired textiles or other objects – was all the rage in seventeenth and eighteenth century Europe.

The rise of landscape painting during the Song dynasty added a new dimension to textile art, which began to follow the style and composition of brush painting. Actual copies were made of the paintings of masters. *Ke-si* was often woven in the style of landscape and bird-and-flower paintings, and embroidery too now followed the painterly style. Complex, colorful, and varied, these were paintings by inspired weavers and needleworkers.

Tapestry landscape painting, Ming dynasty

"Raising Silkworms," a contemporary peasant painting, Huxian

SILK MAKING: TECHNIQUES AND MATERIALS

MAKING SILK THREAD

Silk is an animal fiber made from the cocoon of the silkworm. The silkworm eggs are carefully incubated for twelve days. When they hatch into tiny larvae, thin as hair, they are placed on bamboo trays and fed only fresh mulberry leaves. For the next twenty four to twenty eight days, the delicate little creatures eat constantly; they must be fed fresh leaves as often as every two hours, night and day. Finally the silkworms spin their cocoons of fine thread, which are sent to a filature after three to five days, where they are boiled to dissolve the sticky substance (sericin) that surrounds the thread. The long, fine, continuous fiber is then unreeled in one continuous length, ready for dyeing and weaving.

About two-fifths of the silk produced in the world today comes from China; the principal areas of production are east central Jiangsu and Zhejiang provinces. Guangdong, in the south, has only a small breeding area, but can produce as many as seven generations of worms in one year, compared with the one or two generations raised in other areas. Until 1950 silkworms were raised only in peasant households, without benefit of the discoveries which had made sericulture in other lands forge ahead. Today scientific breeding methods are replacing the hit-or-miss techniques of the past, but mulberry leaves still must be gathered by hand, and raising silkworms is still a labor-intensive process. Sericulture and the production of silk thread have ranked in importance with agriculture in Chinese history. Thus, modernizing the industry is an important goal in China today.

WEAVING: TECHNIQUES AND MATERIALS

Cloth is woven on a loom – a simple frame or a very complex automatic machine. Drawlooms, invented in China, permit the weaving of intricate patterns. Warp threads enter the loom lengthwise and weft threads move over and under the warp to create the cloth. There are thousands of possible combinations of warp and weft threads, especially when weaving with fine silk.

In a simple or plain "tabby" weave, one weft thread moves over one warp thread and under the next in a continuous movement. Even this simple stitch will produce different effects if the threads are lighter or heavier or if the warp and weft have different weights or textures. Brocades and damasks are fabrics that have patterns woven in the cloth. In damask the design can be read on both the front and back. A brocade may have a simple tabby weave background with a contrasting pattern of birds and flowers in a satin weave.

The art of weaving lies in creating patterns through the almost endless possibilities of the loom – adding color, inlaying designs of flowers or figures as in brocade, or mixing weaves. Some weaving effects created thousands of years ago have been lost over the ages; modern researchers are trying to reconstruct the techniques. New styles have also come into being as modern technology has increased the artistic possibilities of the loom.

TRADITIONAL WEAVING CENTERS

Suzhou

In Suzhou, Jiangsu Province, an imperial weaving workshop was founded in the Ming dynasty to create the emperor's dragon robes. Thousands of looms operated over the centuries in Suzhou, located in the heart of China's silk-producing region. The exquisite brocades made for the imperial household have given the city a reputation for the finest artistry. Suzhou handweavers are also accomplished in the art of tapestry.

Hangzhou

Hangzhou, in Zhejiang Province, is also located in silk country and was the site of an imperial brocade workshop. Hangzhou weavers are famous for creating rainbow-hued damasks, filmy, flowered, sheer silks, and satin brocades threaded with gold. After 1950, designers studied the brocade-weaving techniques of the Tang, Song, and Ming dynasties to recapture the best of the old. Today they are experimenting with new silk weaves, raised patterning, embroidered effects, and the use of colored metallic thread for interweaving. Reproductions of famous paintings, wall hangings, and fine tapestries are also woven in Hangzhou.

Nanjing

Nanjing, Jiangsu Province, produces brocades using gold and silver threads. Here, too, silk has been woven for centuries, and an imperial factory was established in the city during the Ming. After 1950, modern handweavers received help from artists sent to copy ancient designs.

Chengdu

Chengdu, Sichuan Province, is called the "City of Brocade." The Brocade River, which runs through the city, is so called because the famous Shu brocades were washed in its waters. A silk weaving and embroidery workshop was established in the city over fifteen hundred years ago. Present-day Chengdu has studied its design traditions and is once again famous for its classic, colorful woven styles.

EMBROIDERY: TECHNIQUES AND MATERIALS

Embroidery probably originated soon after the discovery of silk. The earliest embroidered fabrics are executed in a simple chain stitch, but as early as two thousand years ago, during the Han dynasty, at least eight embroidery stitches had already come into use. (Today there are probably as many as forty different embroidery stitches.) Han records reveal that embroidery was preferred to brocade, since embroidery produced more colorful effects. Embroidery was sometimes added to woven brocades and damasks, especially in imperial dragon robes.

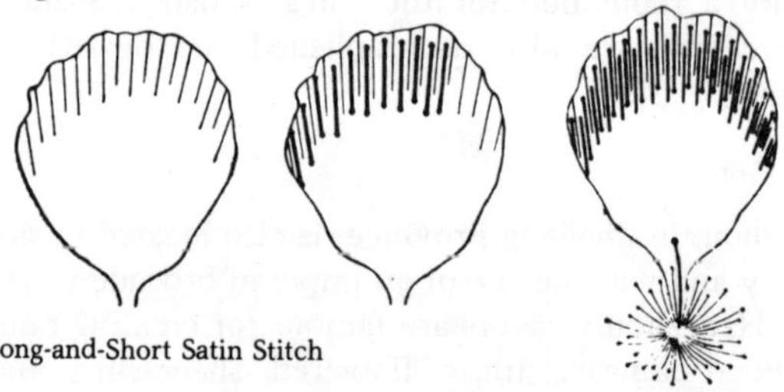

Long-and-Short Satin Stitch

Satin Stitch

Satin stitch is a closely packed straight stitch which produces an even, smooth, flat surface. Long and short satin stitches are used to give shading to a pattern. For this reason satin stitches are used to copy paintings or create a painted effect. The needle is used like a brush; long and short strokes blend tones and colors. The satin stitch is basic to all Chinese embroidery and is used with several variations. The slant of the stitch is determined by the pattern. When the silk floss is slanted in various directions, it catches the light in different ways and an effect of toning is achieved. Satin stitch is used exclusively in two-sided embroidery, where the stitch is exactly the same on both sides of the design. An extremely long satin stitch sometimes floats or covers an unusually large area; the stitch is then "couched," or held down. Satin stitch may also be padded, or worked over a coarser stitch, to create a relief effect.

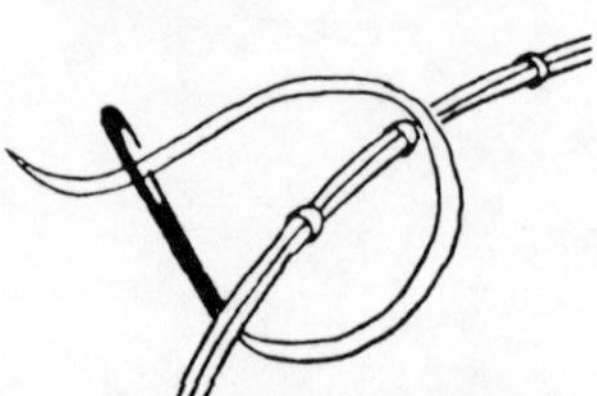

Couching Stitch

Couching stitch is used to hold gold or silver threads in place. Gold thread, used to outline the animal motifs on mandarin squares or the dragons on imperial robes, was made by winding gold leaf around a thin, silk core. The couching stitch is almost invisible. The lavish taste of the late Ming and Qing called for a great deal of gold and silver thread, not only for outline, but as spirals and other geometric motifs.

Stem stitch is used for outlining flower stems, especially in conjunction with the smooth, even satin stitches used for flower petals. The stem stitch is used to outline a design.

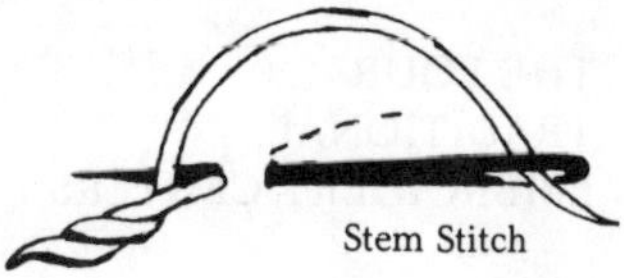

Stem Stitch

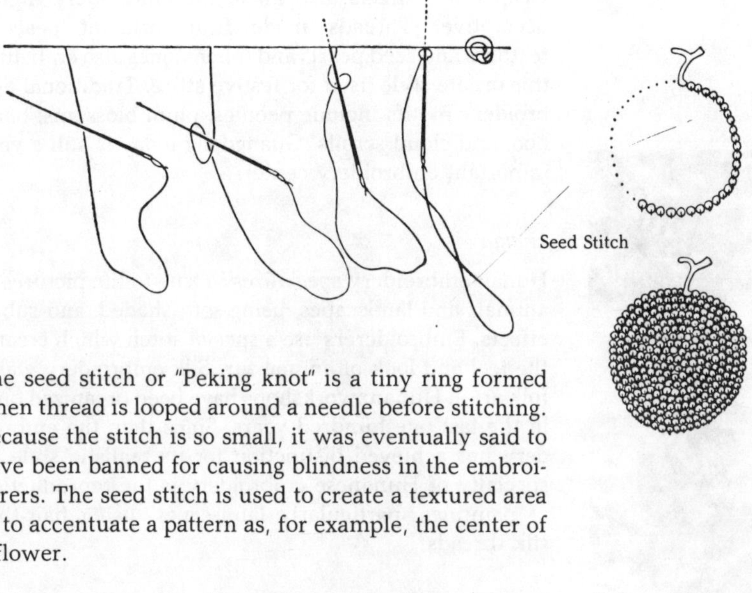

Seed Stitch

The seed stitch or "Peking knot" is a tiny ring formed when thread is looped around a needle before stitching. Because the stitch is so small, it was eventually said to have been banned for causing blindness in the embroiderers. The seed stitch is used to create a textured area or to accentuate a pattern as, for example, the center of a flower.

Textures are produced by twisting and plying yarns, as well as by using specific stitches that dot or outline. Silk yarns are very fine, but they may be split to become even finer. In double-sided embroidery the thread is split many times.

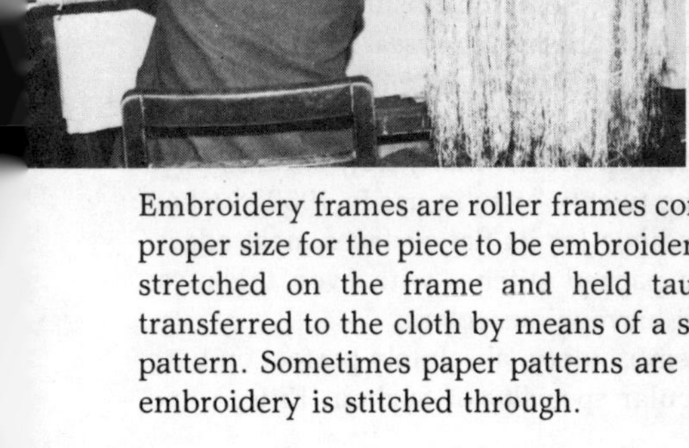

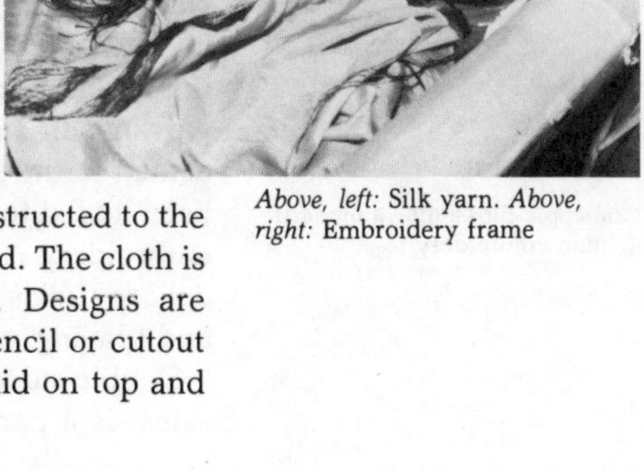

Above, left: Silk yarn. *Above, right:* Embroidery frame

Embroidery frames are roller frames constructed to the proper size for the piece to be embroidered. The cloth is stretched on the frame and held taut. Designs are transferred to the cloth by means of a stencil or cutout pattern. Sometimes paper patterns are laid on top and embroidery is stitched through.

THE FOUR TRADITIONAL EMBROIDERY CENTERS

Guangdong

The Guangdong or "Yue" style of embroidery flourished during the Tang and Ming. This flamboyant style uses gold and silver thread and rich shades of red and green. Deep relief effects also make the embroidery highly decorative. Threads made from brilliant peacock feathers and seed pearls and other stones also embellish this ornate style used for festive attire. Traditional embroidery motifs include peonies, plum blossoms, bamboo, and cloud scrolls. Guangdong today is still a very important embroidery center.

"Crabapple Blossoms," a modern Sichuan embroidery

Hunan

Hunan embroidery specializes in true-to-life pictures of animals and landscapes, using soft, shaded, and subtle effects. Embroiderers use a special stitch which creates the feel and look of animal fur. Silk embroidery was a folk art in Hunan; workshops have been organized only in the last one hundred years. Since then the embroidery has achieved distinction for its realistic style. A specialty of Hunanese embroidery is the reproduction of paintings, particularly landscapes, using hair-thin silk threads.

Sichuan

Sichuan specializes in the embroidery of large squares for quilts and household goods. Weaving and embroidery were first established in Sichuan over fifteen hundred years ago, making this one of China's earliest textile centers.

Suzhou

Located in Jiangsu Province, in the heart of silk-producing country, Suzhou has been renowned for silk weaving and embroidery for centuries. It is, in addition, a center for over forty different handicrafts. Today the National Embroidery Research Institute is situated here, with a design workshop to research the past and improve and modernize the art of embroidery. Handwoven silk tapestries of the highest artistry are executed in the research center. Many new stitches have been added to the twenty or so in use in 1950. Suzhou embroidery is famous for its flat surfaces, neat edges, delicacy, closely packed stitches with even thickness and spacing, and harmonious colors.

Double-sided embroidery, absolutely perfect on both sides, is a particular specialty of Suzhou. Kittens and

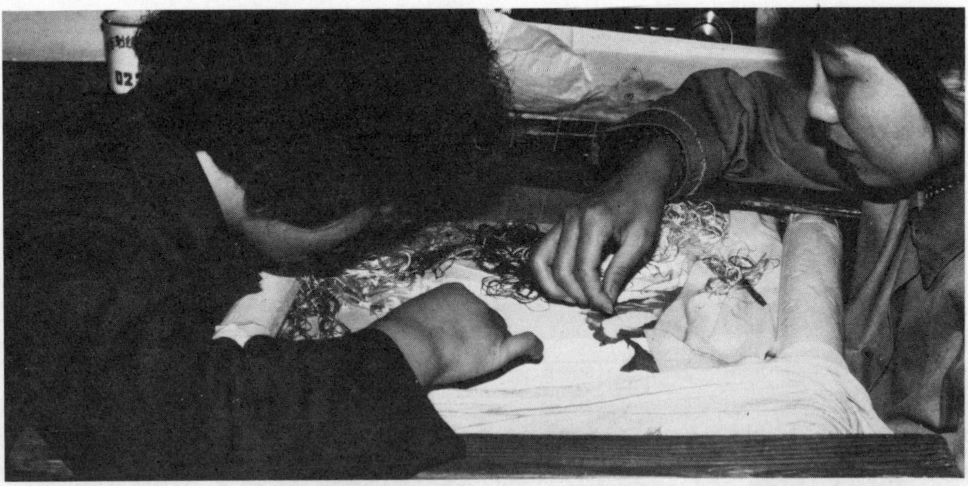

goldfish are traditional subjects still used today. This embroidery requires silk thread much finer than the ordinary, and it is worked on sheets of fine, transparent nylon. Double-sided embroidery has even been executed with different colors on each side.

The life of master embroiderer Jin Qingfen provides a good example of how the old has met the new in Suzhou. Like most of the women embroiderers of Suzhou, Jin Qingfen learned her craft when she was quite young. By the age of twelve, she had already begun to make her living by helping her mother do piecework farmed out by embroidery shops. After executing a successful piece for the Empress Dowager Ci Xi, she was called to the capital to work for the nobility and teach their daughters the art of embroidery. Jin had a hard life in the unstable years following the fall of the Qing dynasty. After the deaths of her husband and family, she was reduced to working as a house servant. After the founding of the People's Republic in 1949, she was invited to assist in establishing the Suzhou Embroidery Research Institute. Here she recorded the traditional embroidery skills and taught this beautiful art to the younger generation. To the repertoire of traditional subjects such as flowers, birds, and portraits, she added lively scenes from daily life such as transplanting rice shoots.

Double-sided embroidery kittens

FOR FURTHER READING

Cammann, Schuyler. *China's Dragon Robes.* New York: Ronald Press, 1952.

Chung, Young Y. *The Art of Oriental Embroidery.* New York: Scribners, 1979.

Myrdal, Jan. *The Silk Road.* New York: Pantheon, 1979.

Imperial brush pot of carved cinnabar lacquer, Qing dynasty

CHAPTER 7

LACQUERWARE

PRESERVING THE PAST

Lacquer painting, as well as the crafting of beautiful, light, graceful vessels in lacquer, was already an accomplished art over two thousand years ago. The lac tree is native to China and grows wild over the south and central areas. When the marvelous preservative properties of the sap of the tree were discovered, it was quickly used to coat boats, food utensils, weapons, and leather. Artisans found that the glossy substance could be colored and dried to a hard, shiny surface, excellent for decoration. In fact, the best record of early styles of painting comes from thousands of pieces of painted lacquerware which have been found perfectly preserved after being buried over two thousand years ago.

Black and red painted lacquer cup, Changsha, Warring States period

SWIRLING CLOUDS AND FIGHTING DRAGONS

The finest vessels of the Warring States period and later of the Han were an early type of "bodiless lacquer," formed of layers of lacquer applied to a fabric base. Ordinary vessels had a wooden base. In 1971 several hundred pieces of lacquer were uncovered in the tomb of a Han noblewoman at Mawangdui, near Changsha; they are superb examples of early artistic skill. Each tray, cup, box, and utensil is exquisitely decorated with fluid motifs of swirling clouds and spirals, or volutes. Some pieces are of red lacquer painted with black. Others use a black lacquer background to display graceful patterns of white, green, yellow, or red. Jars found in the tomb resemble the bronze shapes of the period, while the painted motifs are similar to those on woven silk and inlaid bronzes. The middle and outer layers of the noblewoman's coffin were lacquered and painted with fantastic beasts; other objects were decorated with dancing birds and upright dragons carrying weapons, which were familiar themes in Han arts and crafts. In addition to small animals caught in midflight, Han lacquers contain some of the earliest paintings of human figures; but it was the playful, mythical animals, often dissolving into the pure energy of abstract spirals of color, that

Fighting dragon, Han dynasty

seem to have provided the Han craftsman with his greatest inspiration.

Lacquer was an important craft industry of the Han and was carefully controlled by the state. At this time Sichuan, with two important imperial factories, was the center of the industry. The costly creations of these factories were sent throughout the empire. Workshops existed in all the central and southern provinces, however, making everyday wares as well as products for court needs. The craft was highly specialized, and as many as eight artisans were needed to create one piece. Separate craftsmen fashioned the wooden base, processed the lacquer, applied the lacquer coatings, made the metal fittings, added the decoration, inscribed the article, and completed the final polishing. One artisan was in charge of the overall work, and numerous officials oversaw the workshops, adding their names to the list of contributing craftsmen inscribed on each ware.

Water dipper with cloud design, Han dynasty

LATER LACQUERWARE: NEW FORMS

Lacquered objects never lost their importance among Chinese crafts in the succeeding centuries. Lacquered wood became especially important because of the perfect protection afforded by the lac. In the Tang, light, bodiless lacquer, in which the central core was removed after the work had dried, was used to create fluid statues of Buddhist figures. The image was first modeled in clay, and then numerous coats of liquid lacquer were added, which exactly reproduced the form of the original. When the lacquer had dried, the clay was removed, leaving a light yet durable sculpture.

By the Tang dynasty, artisans were carving through layers of lacquer to produce intricate designs. Sometimes the layers were pigmented with contrasting colors, so that the relief pattern was variegated. The most popular carved lacquer perfected in the workshops of Beijing was of cinnabar red, with floral motifs or landscape scenes. Tang artisans also developed the technique of mother-of-pearl inlay. Following the ornate style of palace arts in the Ming and Qing, ivory and gold leaf, as well as mother-of-pearl, were inlaid in lacquerware. Whole pictures of pearl inlay decorated chests, screens, and tables of these later periods.

SCREENS FOR EXPORT

In the eighteenth century, screens became a popular export item when trade with the West began to mushroom. Carved screens of lacquer were especially popular, and were often hastily made in Fuzhou or Guangzhou. Instead of using the expensive and time-

Eight panel export screen, Qing dynasty

consuming method of building up hundreds of layers of lacquer, artisans applied a relatively small number of lacquer coatings to a wooden base. The carving style was bold and the exposed areas of the wooden base were given a coat of brightly colored lacquer paint. These were called "Coromandel" screens because they were shipped from China to the Coromandel Coast of southwest India and from there conveyed all over Europe and the West.

Below, left: Carved lacquer, Yuan dynasty. *Below, right:* Carved lacquer plate, Ming dynasty

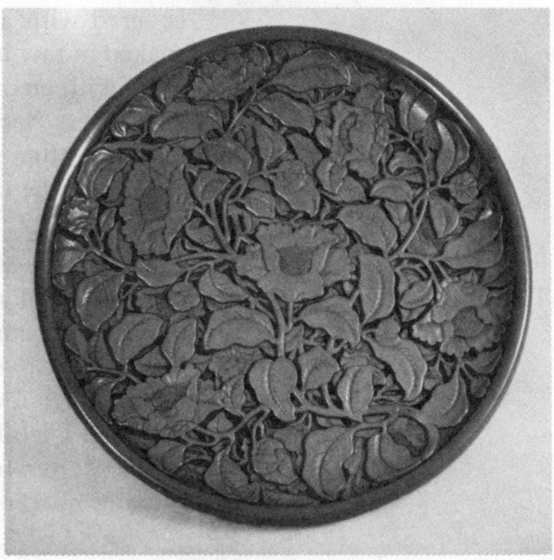

THE DRAGON THRONE

The skilled lacquer craftsmen of the Ming found worthy successors among the imperial artisans in the workshops of the Qian-long emperor. Their skill is exemplified by the superb carved throne created for this eighteenth-century emperor in the imperial lacquer workshop. Exquisitely carved throughout, the throne is primarily red but also has layers of yellow, brown, and two tones of green. The piece is lavishly decorated with symbols of longevity, prosperity, and good fortune, such as an elephant bearing a vase of jewels, a rebus for "peace reigning in the north." This is perhaps the pinnacle of the Chinese lacquer carver's skill.

LACQUERWARE: TECHNIQUES AND MATERIALS

LACQUER

Lacquer comes from the sap of the lac tree, *Rhus verniciflua,* a variety of sumac. On contact with air the sap hardens, producing a coat which is resistant to corrosion, rust, acids, insects, and moisture, thus protecting against disintegration and chemical change. The raw lacquer, or lac, is collected and purified, forming a shiny, transparent liquid. Mineral pigments supply the colors, which are added before the lacquer is sealed in airtight containers. Black and red – from iron and mercury respectively – are the two most important colors of lacquerware. Traditionally red was used for carving and black as a base for painting.

Raw lac

BASE

The base may be either wood or, more usually, copper. The wood is carefully primed and smoothed, and then covered with a silk or hempen cloth which has been soaked in raw lacquer paste. The copper base is usually lined with enamel.

"Bodiless lacquer" is extremely light in weight because, after successive layers of lacquer have been applied to the cloth-covered base, the base is removed.

BUILDING THE LACQUER

Lacquerware is prepared by building up successive layers of lac. Each coat must dry thoroughly in a moist, temperature-controlled, dust-free atmosphere. A piece may require over one hundred coats before being ready for carving; fewer coats are required for incising or painting. Each layer is ground and polished before the next coat is applied; the final layer is polished to a smooth, mirror-like finish ready for final decoration.

LACQUER CARVING

Lacquer carving was developed as early as the Tang, and has been a specialty of Beijing's lacquerware workshops. Between one hundred and two hundred coats of lacquer may be needed, depending on the depth required for the design; at least half-inch walls are usually needed. The elaborately and intricately carved objects traditionally associated with Beijing workshops are of a red color known as cinnabar, whose hue is derived

Carved lacquer bull, Beijing

from the addition of mercuric sulfide to the lac. Some carved wares have several colors in successive layers, and the carving at different depths reveals the various colors. Openwork effects are also popular, as are high and low relief carving. Carving is done before the lacquer completely hardens. Small objects may have a metal base, while wood is usually used in screens and other large pieces.

Lacquer box inlaid with mother-of-pearl, Ming dynasty

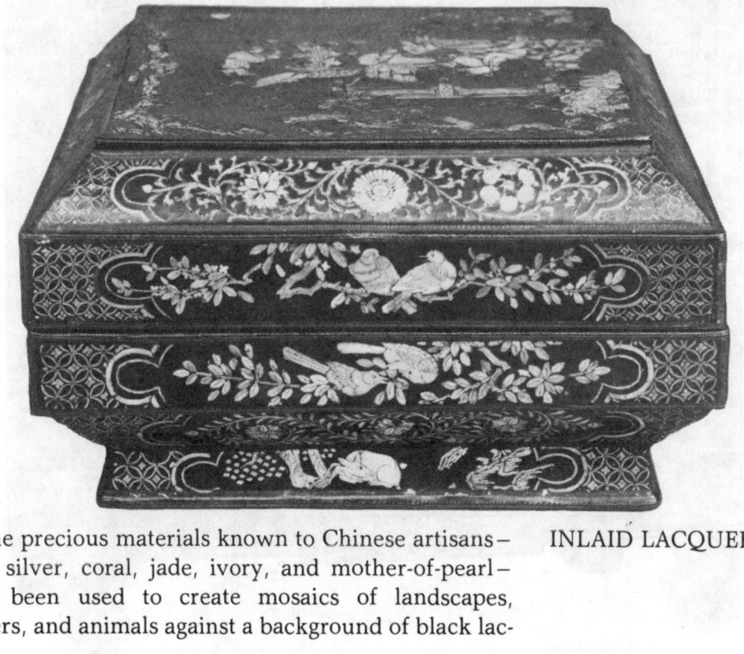

INLAID LACQUERWARE

All the precious materials known to Chinese artisans—gold, silver, coral, jade, ivory, and mother-of-pearl—have been used to create mosaics of landscapes, flowers, and animals against a background of black lacquer. Always used with careful regard for their natural colors, these lacquer inlays are especially popular in screens, cabinets, and other pieces of furniture. They are a specialty of Yangzhou, in Jiangsu Province, which also uses the inlay technique for exquisite small plates and plaques.

PAINTED AND INCISED LACQUERWARE

Lacquer-based paints are used to sketch traditional motifs, such as landscapes, flowers, and animals, usually on a black base. A thin gold outline may frame the

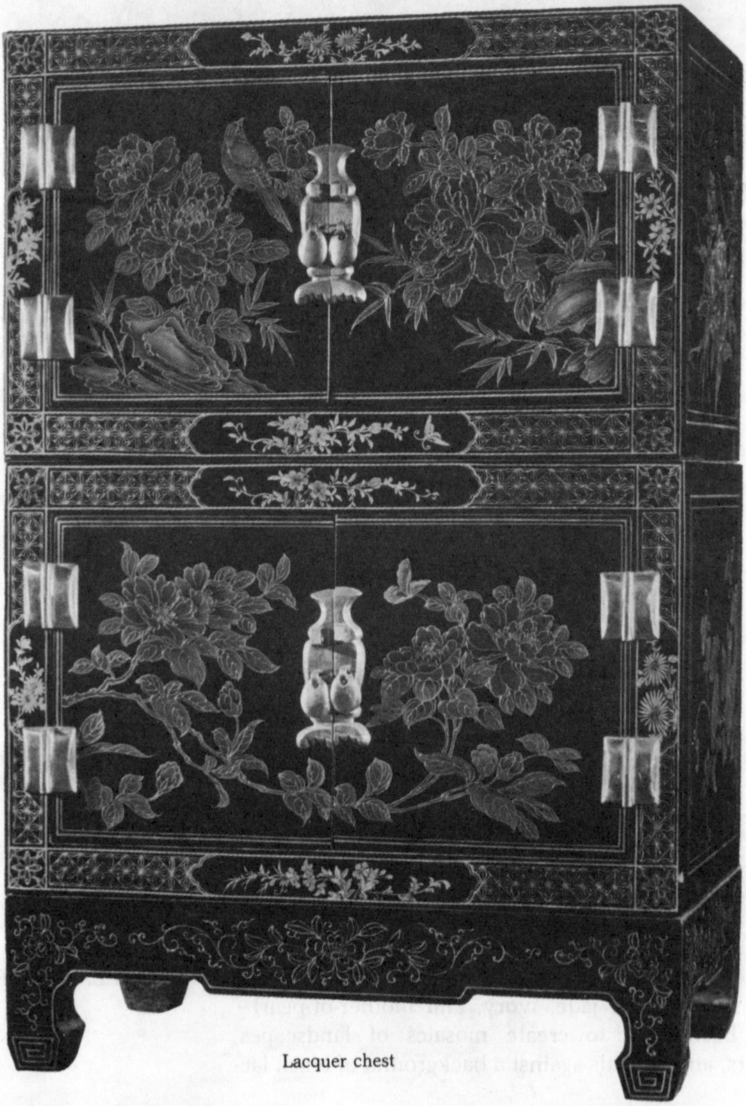

Lacquer chest

painted design, while a thin coat of transparent lacquer provides the final touch. Chongqing and Chengdu, Sichuan Province, were both traditional centers for painted lacquer and continue to be important today.

Incising is another popular lacquer technique. After incising, the pattern lines are filled with silver or gold, or another lacquer color. Many decorative techniques, such as painting, incising, carving, and inlay, are combined in contemporary lacquerware.

FUZHOU: CITY OF LACQUER

In the eighteenth century, bodiless wares were first made in Fuzhou and soon became the specialty of that city. Today the "three treasures" of Chinese crafts are the porcelains of Jingdezhen, Beijing cloisonné, and bodiless lacquers from Fuzhou. The light weight of Fuzhou lacquerware is often astounding. In the Great Hall of the People in Beijing, there are two lions, apparently ancient bronzes, and two enormous red vases. All the pieces could be easily carried by one person, however, and closer inspection reveals that they are actually made of lacquer! *San-cai* and other ceramic glazes have also been imitated in lacquer, as have designs from folk crafts.

Fuzhou bodiless lacquer vase

Today lacquer centers are found in most areas of China. Although many cities specialize in one kind of work, all centers make use of a variety of techniques. Lacquer artisans continue to work to improve their processes and add colors and designs. Today in Fuzhou there are two lacquerware factories with over one thousand workers. The Fujian Provincial Arts and Crafts Research Institute specializes in lacquer and trains workers in this complicated production technique, which often requires as many as forty processes. In addition, industrial applications of lacquer and the use of lacquer to replace heavier materials are being studied.

FOR FURTHER READING

David, Sir Percival. *Chinese Connoisseurship. The Ko ku yao lun. The Essential Criteria of Antiquities.* London: Faber and Faber, 1971.

Garner, Sir Harry. *Chinese Lacquer.* London: Faber and Faber, 1979.

CHAPTER 8

CLOISONNE, METALWORK, AND GLASS

ENAMELWARE: AN ARABIAN ART COMES TO CHINA

The Yuan dynasty was founded by Mongol invaders under the banner of Genghis Khan, and the empire was extended by his sons and his grandson, Kublai. The fabled Khanbalik – present-day Beijing – was the great capital of Kublai Khan visited by Marco Polo in the thirteenth century. The Mongol empire stretched throughout East Asia from Korea and Manchuria in the north to Annam (North Viet Nam) in the south, through Central Asia, Persia, and Russia. The needs of Kublai Khan and his court were served by skilled craftsmen who brought arts and crafts from all over the world. Artisans from Germany, France, Armenia, and other European countries were employed by the Mongol court; often they were prisoners captured during the Mongol campaigns and sent back to serve the Khan. A French goldsmith who had been taken captive in Hungary created elaborate constructions of gold and silver for the court in Khanbalik, thus introducing new techniques to Chinese craftsmen. Arab merchants also carried new ideas and skills from the Middle East to China, including the art of enameling, best known in cloisonné.

CLOISONNE

The art of enameling originated as a substitute form of inlay: instead of using precious and semiprecious stones, enamels as bright as jewels were inlaid in gold ornaments. The first Chinese reference to enamels occurs in 1388 during the early years of the Ming dynasty. A famous and important book on antiquities, called *Ge gu yao lun,* describes the origins and categories of many Chinese crafts, including a brief entry on cloisonné, described as *Da-shi,* or "Moslem" ware; it was also called *Gui-guo yao,* or "ware of the Devil's Country."

The writer of the *Ge gu yao lun* found fault with the ostentatious style of cloisonné, however, saying that the

Opposite: Large cloisonné vase, Ming dynasty

objects he had seen—incense burners, flower vases, round, covered boxes, and wine cups—would only be suitable for use in the women's quarters and would be entirely inappropriate for the restrained setting of the scholar's studio. In spite of such criticism, the vivid colors of cloisonné were soon adapted to suit traditional craft styles, and these ornate and bright wares gained great popularity.

From the beginning cloisonné must have received the patronage of the court or the very rich, as the craft required rare and precious materials and involved a highly technical process of production. In fact almost all cloisonné was made in Beijing, which is the home of China's cloisonné workshops today.

Below: Ritual bronze wine vessel, Shang dynasty. *Below, right:* Cloisonné censer, Ming dynasty

AWESOME BRONZES: THE EARLIEST CHINESE METALWORK

The art of the Chinese bronze caster is very ancient. About four thousand years ago the lovely shapes evolved by Neolithic potters were first adapted for use in bronze. The bronze caster refined old ceramic forms and added new ones, creating vessels for use in ritual sacrifices to the royal ancestors: imposing wine containers with sharply jutting flanges and monumental food and cooking vessels with high relief decoration. Early bronze art is awesome and greatly stylized; its ritual function is very clear. Mystical animal masks, plumed birds, coiling dragons, and other zoomorphic motifs set amid thunder patterns and abstract designs cover the surfaces of cast bronzes so technically accomplished that they have never been surpassed.

About the middle of the first millennium BC, however, these massive bronzes with their frightening animals began to disappear. The metal shapes became streamlined and elegant, decorated with fluid cloud spirals, wave patterns, and geometric designs. The spirals were superbly enhanced by inlays of silver, gold, copper, turquoise, and malachite.

THE BEAUTIFUL BLUES OF MING CLOISONNE

The art of inlaid bronze was already centuries old when enameled wares were first imported from Arabia. Chinese artisans quickly adapted the enameling process to the old bronze craft, and by the early fifteenth century Ming craftsmen had created a special look, using two distinctive enamel colors—a turquoise derived from native mineral pigments and an imported cobalt blue.

The earliest cloisonné motifs included cloud patterns and scrolls of lotus and *ling-zhi*, followed later by dragons amid clouds, florals, landscapes, and human and animal figures. The vivid colors of the enamels suited the change in aesthetic from the quiet and subtle shades of the Song to the more robust tastes of the later Yuan and Ming courts. The designs of Ming cloisonné are bold and simple, and wares were often created in imitation of antique bronzes. As the techniques of cloisonné were still being perfected in the Ming, wares often reveal a rough surface with imperfectly filled cells.

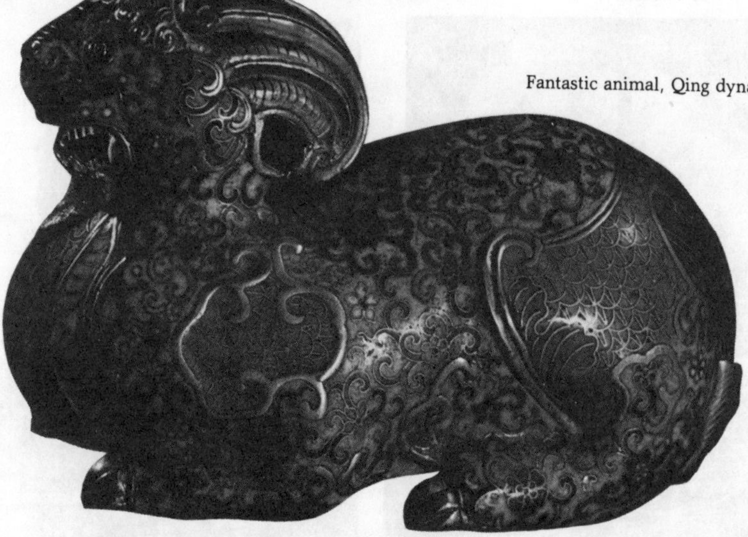

Fantastic animal, Qing dynasty

IMPERIAL WORKSHOPS OF THE SEVENTEENTH AND EIGHTEENTH CENTURIES

In 1680 the Kang-xi emperor established imperial workshops in Beijing for the manufacture of cloisonné, resulting in a noticeable improvement in quality. During the reign of the Qian-long emperor in the eighteenth century, Chinese craftsmen achieved the delicacy of execution and polished finish which characterize the best of today's wares. Thin copper ribbons were deftly fashioned to create amazingly intricate and beautiful floral designs, with stems and leaves interwoven in smooth, fluid lines. Brilliant flowers were set within the deep cobalt blue background so popular at the time, and the contrast was further enhanced by a richly decorative gilt outline. Cloisonné enamelware had reached technical perfection.

The palace workshops of the seventeenth and eighteenth centuries also produced objects of gold and silver for court use. Since the fifth century, Chinese silver and goldsmiths had begun to adapt Sassanian techniques and designs which had come over the Silk Road from the Middle East. Delicate etchings of lotuses, peonies, and animal motifs basic to Chinese art were often combined with elements of Persian style. Gold and silver bowls were fashioned in the shape of a flower, each petal formed in repoussé (hammered from the back to create a relief). Later gold ornaments and jewelry made extensive use of filigree and inlay of semiprecious stones. In the Qing, Manchu noblewomen wore elaborate headdresses of gilded silver filigree on a metal foundation inset with semiprecious stones. Brilliant

Below: Silver cups, Yuan dynasty.
Below, left: Bronze lion

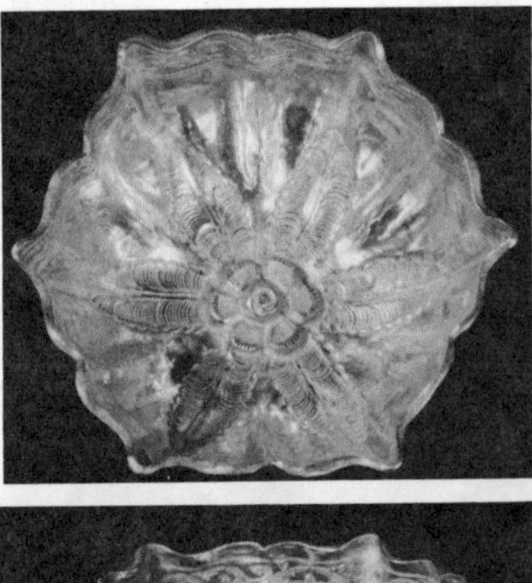

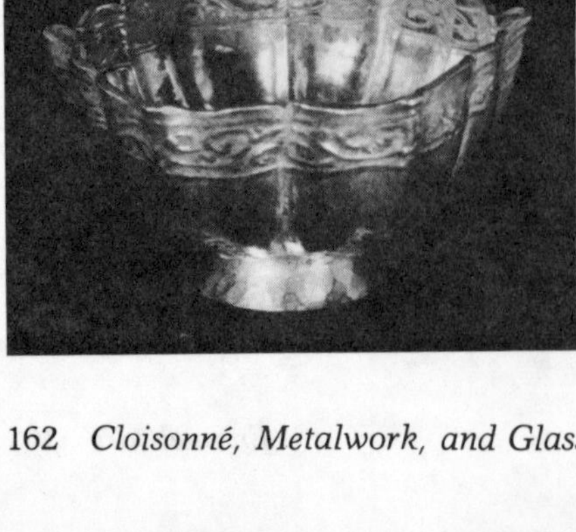

blue-green kingfisher feathers added the final touch of opulence. Ornate headdresses of kingfisher feathers and gilded silver filigree also formed part of the official costume of the Qing emperors.

Today the techniques of the silversmiths of the Qing imperial workshops have been revived. Beijing is again the center of the metalwork industry, and craft workers create fantastic dragons, phoenixes, horses, and human figures of solid gold or gold and silver filigree inset with coral, amethyst, pearls, rubies, and turquoise. Beijing is also renowned for its fine gold and silver jewelry, encrusted with polished semiprecious stones set in *cabochon,* or unfaceted, style.

Below, left: Modern filigree and inlay. *Below:* Inspecting cloisonné flower vases

TODAY'S CLOISONNE: A SPECIALTY OF BEIJING

As was the case with all China's arts and crafts, cloisonné declined in the early twentieth century, so that only eighty craftsmen were left in Beijing in the 1950s when the People's Republic of China began to organize small cooperatives to revive the old craft. A state experimental workshop was soon established to study design and technique, and the cooperatives merged to form the present Beijing Cloisonné Studio, whose two thousand workers are today housed in a large, modern building.

The old skills are still evident. One old master craftsman can twist copper wire into a hundred varieties of chrysanthemums, while another can fashion two dragons playing ball, all within the space of a tiny

Modern cloisonné vessel with silver dragon and bird decoration

cloisonné finger ring. New enamel shades have been added to increase the subtlety of available colors, and reproductions of classic paintings are now executed in cloisonné.

Modern cloisonné is an important Chinese export. Traditional shapes are still popular, including cranes, horses, *fu* lions, rabbits, camels, and elephants. Wares are made to serve as candlesticks, wine sets, teapots, vases, bowls, plates, jars, ashtrays, covered boxes, napkin rings, salt and pepper sets, bracelets, rings, screens, and hanging panels. Painted enamels on metal are also fashioned as teapots, cups, and other items, but their popularity has never approached that of cloisonné in China. Cloisonné is once again numbered among the export specialties of Beijing, where production has greatly increased in the past 30 years.

CLOISONNE AND ENAMELWARE: TECHNIQUES AND MATERIALS

The enameling process is essentially the adhesion of glass to metal, two substances of very different physical properties. Unlike ceramic glazes, an enamel surface does not fuse with its metal base, but only adheres to it. Thus the enamel artisan must exercise great skill in order to marry these two disparate elements.

Applying enamel colors

Enamel is formed of glass, itself a simple compound of silica (sand) mixed with small amounts of soda, lime, borax, and potash to lower the temperature at which it fuses. When the molten glass base is being used for enamels, it is called a "frit." Metallic oxides as colorants are added to the molten frit, which is then cooled and ground to a fine powder.

ENAMEL COLORS

Popular colors during the Ming dynasty included turquoise, cobalt blue, black, green, red, yellow, and purple. Additional colors were obtained by grinding and mixing several colors. The final powder was mixed with water to make a paste. Mixing and fusing the colored granules was considered an art in itself. Rose pink, derived from gold, was added to the enamel palette only in the eighteenth century; today over forty colors are available to the artist. The fired enamel may be transparent, like colored glass, translucent, or opaque. Opaque enamel, which is often used for painted enamelware, is formed by adding tin oxide to the frit. Because of their varied components, different colors have different firing temperatures, neccssitating repeated firings beginning with those of higher melting points.

TYPES OF ENAMELWARE

Cloisonné

Cloisonné wares are made of closed cells or partitions, formed of thin wires of bronze or copper, and filled with enamel paste. The wire cloisons (partitions) act to separate the colors and may vary in thickness, depending on the design. They are shaped into intricate patterns and attached by adhesive to a copper base hammered into the desired form. The wires are then per-

Forming wire cells

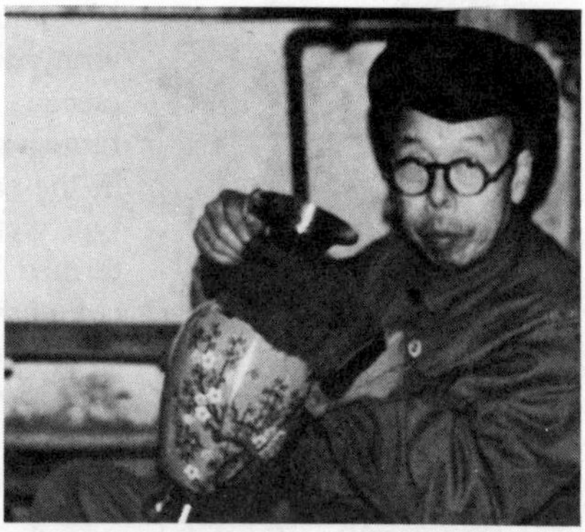

Above, left: Firing the ware.
Above: Polishing the final product

manently fused to the base by solder, which is dusted over the surface. The cloisons are filled with colored enamel pastes, and fired after the pastes have dried. As the enamels contract in firing, several fillings and firings may be necessary to produce the final thickness. After firing, the surface is ground to a smooth finish with carborundum or other abrasives, and then polished with powdered charcoal. The copper wires are gilded, a process now done by electroplate. This gold plating adds radiance to the final design.

The metal base may take any desired shape. It can be hammered to form a vase, a lamp base, jewelry, boxes, and so forth. The filled cloisons are essentially the decoration of the metal form. Although the earliest cloisonné bases were of cast bronze, lighter and more malleable sheet copper was adopted by the early sixteenth century. The earliest wires were carefully and laboriously hammered from slabs of bronze. Wire drawing was imported from the West in the early seventeenth century, and copper wire substituted for bronze.

Champlevé

Champlevé is a type of enamelware in which depressions are carved out of the metal background and filled with enamels. The pattern is formed by the carving, and colored enamels are used to fill the cavities.

Repoussé

Repoussé enamelware is formed by hammering cavities into the metal base; the cavities are then filled as in champlevé.

Painted Enamelware

Called "foreign porcelain" (*yang-ci*) in Chinese, these metal-based wares are covered with a continuous coat of opaque enamel, usually white. A design is painted on with additional coats of colored enamel and then the piece is fired. The technique was developed initially at Limoges in France and was probably imported to China in the early eighteenth century. Chinese wares of this type were usually painted at Guangzhou and were thus termed "Canton enamels." The bulk of this work was commissioned by Western traders for export; European motifs and emblems such as coats of arms and religious scenes were frequently seen on these wares. Porcelain and metal enamelwares often have similar colors and motifs.

Snuff bottles

GLASS

Skill at glassmaking came rather late to China. Glass was first imported about the middle of the first millennium BC, when ingots from the Near East were carried to China and reworked into ornamental beads and discs. The colored glass was valued primarily as a substitute for rare and semiprecious stones, especially jade. One tomb excavation turned up a funerary cicada made of glass, instead of the traditional jade, to be placed on the tongue of the corpse. The production of lead glazes during the Han proves that Chinese craftsmen knew the technique of vitrification. However, the artisans were absorbed in creating glass-like glazes for their already sophisticated ceramics and stoneware. The techniques of glassmaking itself did not become widespread until the fifth century. Even at that time glass was usually shaped in colors and forms imitating semiprecious stones.

During the Ming dynasty objects of opaque glass such

Snuff bottles

as bottles, vases, and bowls were produced in Boshan (now called Zibo), Shandong Province. Such pieces were covered with a layer of colored glass and carved in a special cameo technique. In the late seventeenth century, the first imperial glass workshop was established in Beijing to serve the court of the Kang-xi emperor, and bars of colored glass were imported from Boshan to be reworked at the imperial factory. Glass was a popular medium for the elaborately painted "snuff bottles" so popular during the Qing dynasty. Originally designed to hold medicines, these bottles were carved in cameo technique or decorated with painted enamels and were considered a specialty of the Beijing workshops. Late in the Qing, the art of backpainting was used to decorate the interior of the transparent glass snuff bottles. Incredibly detailed miniature paintings of landscapes, flowers, animals, or even whole genre scenes were painted inside the tiny, transparent bottles. This technique of interior painting (*nei-hua*) is still a specialty of Beijing; it is practiced today in the Beijing Arts and Crafts Institute and the workshops of the Beijing branch of the Arts and Crafts Import and Export Corporation. Zibo has also maintained its status as a major glass center and today includes ceramics, as well as cameo glasswares, among its products.

FOR FURTHER READING

Garner, Sir Harry. *Chinese and Japanese Cloisonné Enamels.* Rutland, VT: C.E. Tuttle, 1962.

A folk batik print by Yu Wuzhang

CHAPTER 9

FOLK AND REGIONAL ARTS

A village woman in Hunan plaits thin strips of bamboo to make a sleeping mat; in Weifang an old worker lovingly follows bold outlines to carve woodblocks for colorful New Year pictures. In Wuxi the grandson of an old craftsman molds dolls and animals from clay to make characters from classic operas and famous legends; in Yunnan a young girl of the Yi nationality embroiders vividly colored cloud and floral designs on a bag of handwoven hemp. In each of these regions, and all over China, folk art specialties built on rich traditions have been handed down from generation to generation.

These folk artists are practical, and their objects usually develop out of daily necessity. Artistic vision goes into the best of their creations. They have a profound understanding of their materials, which include anything available regionally, from bamboo and dough to boxwood and soapstone.

Colorful, vigorous, and substantial, folk art reflects the life of the common people, their proximity to the earth and its creatures. Their designs are not analytical, but are richly symbolic. Theirs is a different aesthetic from the polished elegance of the palace crafts. Art connoisseurs and historians are just beginning to recognize the beauty and value of folk art, as many crafts in the West are now on the verge of extinction.

Chinese folk art was disdained by the well educated gentleman and the wealthy city merchant. Because history was recorded by the literate elite, who had no interest in folk wares, little is known of the development of these objects. Only since 1949 have designers and professors begun to preserve and study the great variety of Chinese folk crafts, which range from papercuts, woodblock prints, and lanterns to kites, fans, clothing, toys, parasols, and carvings. Some of these goods were created for everyday use and others for use at special events such as festivals or weddings, but even the most mundane bamboo basket or bolt of handprinted cloth bore the personal mark of its maker.

HOLIDAY CRAFTS

Many folk arts were created especially for use during the traditional Chinese festivals. These holidays marked the changes of seasons, which were so important in peasant life. China's economy was based almost entirely on agriculture for thousands of years and has remained so into the modern era. Life was regulated by the farming seasons, punctuated by numerous holidays. The lunar calendar guided farmers in their planting and reaping.

The calendar used at the imperial court and in the cities, however, was solar. The emperor alone could set the official calendar, and in this way he was supposed to attune the human world to the natural order. He renewed the earth each year by ritual plowing, and the empress by ritual sericulture. Festivals, too, were thought to renew the forces of the earth and dispel evil influences.

The most important festival of the year was the New Year, which came at the beginning of the lunar year and stretched through to the Spring Festival in the middle of the first lunar month. This was a time of family reunion when members gathered from all over the country. While the mother prepared large quantities of special boiled dumplings, enough to last for many days, the children cleaned, swept, and set the house in order. The family repaired old utensils and pasted up fresh oiled papers to cover the windows.

PAPERCUTS

At the time of the Spring Festival, parents and children together cut delicate and colorful pictures from thin sheets of paper. These papercut designs, also called window flowers, were pasted on walls and ceilings. When tacked against window papers, the window flowers made a striking contrast of light and shadow. Papercuts also added a festive touch to fans, lanterns, and gifts at this time. Simple utensils were used: special knives or scissors with large, semicircular handles. Ten or more sheets of paper were cut at one time. Sometimes colored paper was chosen, or the fine, absorbent white *xuan* paper which was used for painting. Thin tissue paper was placed between the main sheets to keep the cutting outlines sharp. A rectangular wooden frame with wax panels made a sturdy base for the cutting knife.

In a farming family, papercut patterns could be handed down from generation to generation. Butterfly, peony, chrysanthemum, and bat designs were used by peasant women for both papercuts and embroidery. These patterns served as stencils for making porcelain and lacquer and dyeing textiles, as well as outlines for carving. In spite of this broad repertoire of patterns, however, the most skilled paper cutters worked freehand. In seconds they could create intricate lattice designs or floral motifs.

Contemporary papercuts

Hand coloring contemporary papercuts

No one knows exactly how papercuts began, but they were well known in the Tang over one thousand years ago. Today each region of China specializes in a characteristic type of papercut. Those of the north – Shanxi, Shaanxi, and Shandong – are vigorous and sharp, with bold outlines. The southern styles are more delicate, intricate, and colorful. Foshan, near Guangzhou, is especially famous for its lattice pictures of landscapes and human figures, and florals made of multicolored paper and gold or silver foil. In Guangxi, artists recreate the fantastic peaks of Guilin in charming papercuts. All of these decorations add to the happiness of family celebrations and reunions during the Spring Festival, now celebrated at the time of the lunar New Year.

NEW YEAR PICTURES

Along with the new papercuts prepared during this season, colorful woodblock prints were tacked on both sides of the courtyard gate, on doors, walls, and windows, and over the bed. Called *nian-hua* (New Year pictures) or *men-hua* (door pictures), these prints were very old folk specialties, dating back at least three hundred and fifty years. The most famous centers for New Year pictures were Weifang in Shandong, Yangliuqing in Hebei, and Taohuawu in Jiangsu, although every province had villages which specialized in the craft. In contrast to the refined style of the cities, these prints have a robust style and use bold colors, usually of vegetable origin. Villagers used one block to print a black outline, and then filled in the colors by hand. In later years several blocks were cut to transfer each of the colors of the print. The patterns for the blocks were passed from father to son, in the best craft tradition.

Favorite subjects were heroes from classic novels and operas. Fearsome door gods (*men-shen*) were also put up to frighten away ghosts; dressed in armor and carrying sword and spear, these fierce figures represented the two faithful warriors of a Tang emperor. Because of their loyalty, the emperor is said to have had their pictures painted on the doors of his palace, thus beginning the custom of door gods. Everyone recognized these symbols and the stories they told. Lively pictures of rosy-cheeked children among fish, lotuses, and pomegranates expressed hopes for good fortune and many sons, while scenes of pines and cranes represented a wish for longevity. Crowing roosters welcomed the sunrise, and spirited tigers brought their strength to the household. Farming calendars with local earth gods were also very popular.

Soon the villages evolved strong local styles. The New Year pictures printed in Taohuawu were noted for their delicate shapes and three-dimensional effects. Weifang and Yangliuqing became famous for their exuberant colors and bold, exaggerated shapes. Yangliuqing used a technique combining printing and hand painting, while Weifang developed the use of multiple blocks.

The prints of Yangliuqing were noted for their lively human figures and strong primary colors. Their rather flat style is enhanced by carefully arranged decoration and minute details. The prints became so popular during the Qing dynasty that nearly every family in Yangliuqing made them, and residents of faraway villages came to buy them. In the week before the New Year, the usually peaceful town was crowded with buyers from early morning until late at night. Prints were displayed everywhere – on trees, tables, walls, and carts – and at night they were lit by lanterns, so that sales could continue.

Today, these New Year prints still festoon Chinese villages at Spring Festival time. Pictures of plump children playing with huge peaches and lotuses set the towns ablaze with color. Though now devoid of their superstitious meanings, pictures of door guardians still appear; today's heroes and heroines are as often village workers as legendary figures. Since 1949 many old symbols have been re-created in new form. One par-

New Year picture

ticularly delightful print depicts the old legend of the carp leaping the rapids at Longmen to become a dragon. The carp used to symbolize a scholar who passed the government exams and became a great success. In the modern print a mighty carp, with muscles taut and scales flashing, leaps over the sluice gates of a new dam. The picture points out that hydroelectric power and modernization will be the keys to China's future achievements.

LANTERNS

At the end of the Spring Festival holiday in the middle of the first lunar month came the Lantern Festival. During this holiday every house was lit with brightly colored lanterns of all shapes and sizes. Kindling the lanterns was thought to bring light back to the world at the end of the long winter. The lanterns, hung by doorways, turned night into day. Strollers carried lovely lantern creations with tassels, pearl ornaments, bright feathers, or jade pendants which tinkled as they swayed. Some lanterns were shaped as birds, animals, flowers, boats, or buildings. The famous "galloping horse lanterns" (*zou-ma deng*) spun round and round when a lit candle was placed inside, heating air to turn a hidden wheel. Revolving panels of the "magic lanterns" often told a story, such as the tale of Monkey conquering a horrible demon.

During the Lantern Festival imperial mansions and noble households were lit by costly and elaborate palace lanterns fashioned of silk or glass panels over frames of mahogany, boxwood, or sandalwood. The peasants created less costly but equally colorful lanterns from panels of oiled paper, silk, or sheepskin, fastened to bases of wood, bamboo, wire, or rice stalks. Paintings, embroidery, or papercuts added a bold, festive touch. In the bitter cold of north China peasants even made lanterns by refreezing layer upon layer of ice. When lit with red candles and strung amid the pines, these lanterns cast a charming crystalline glow.

Lanterns

Today lanterns are used to celebrate the Spring Festival and other national holidays such as May Day and National Day (October 1). Red lanterns, hung in city squares and commune courtyards, mark these happy occasions, which are completed with parades and fireworks. Today there is no superstitious meaning behind the use of lanterns, just a rich association with happiness and celebration. The lanterns of Suzhou, shaped of painted silk stretched around frames of sandalwood, boxwood, and mahogany, continue to be admired for their elegance. Foshan, Luoyang, Chengdu, and Shanghai specialize in colorful silk or paper folk lanterns shaped as dragons, phoenixes, lions, or cranes.

WEDDING CRAFTS

The most important ceremony in a girl's life was her wedding, and all her skill went into making her wedding costume and trousseau. Chinese brides often wore embroidered red outer garments. From the age of eight or nine a peasant girl practiced the art of making fine woven cloth and delicate embroidery. She learned her skills from her mother and expected to pass them on to her own daughter in turn. Girls of minority tribes also spent years making their wedding and festival costumes, decorating shoes, sash, hem, and sleeves with vivid panels of embroidery. Floral and animal cross-stitch embroidery and outlines of bold, geometric patterns stood out against handwoven and block print backgrounds. Sometimes fuzzy pieces of silkworm cocoons were even sewn into their designs. Miao girls of southwest China customarily embroidered a sash and presented it to their husbands-to-be. Whether of Han or minority descent, girls refined and modified patterns to create their own effects. Skill at needlework was a source of pride and status, and a girl might wear her wedding costume at festive occasions for the rest of her life. It is no wonder that she took such care in each stitch.

Another folk craft associated with weddings is the wedding box, used to store a girl's trousseau. Every locality had one town or one group of artisans who specialized in this handicraft. Together with the other pieces of the bride's dowry, the wedding boxes, often of polished wood decorated with colorful designs, were carried in a procession through the streets from the bride's to the bridegroom's house, so that all the villagers could view the wealth and domestic skills of the bride. Today the colorful patterns of the wedding boxes are re-created in woodblock prints.

EVERYDAY CRAFTS

BAMBOO

In the warm climate of Jiangxi, Guangdong, Fujian, Zhejiang, and Hunan, lush groves of bamboo cover the earth with a latticework of green. Durable and pliant, the bamboo is a perfect material for making the many necessary articles of daily use, from umbrellas, hats, baskets, and bags, to chairs, chests, and beds. Over the centuries the skilled hands and experienced eyes of folk artists turned common bamboo into works of great beauty.

Making bamboo baskets

Each region has developed its own stylistic features and plaiting techniques. In the subtropical coastal province of Fujian, bamboo grows abundantly, providing an inexhaustible resource for the weaving craft. Families living along the banks of the Yangzi River have used bamboo in their handicrafts for centuries. Stems are heated so that they can be bent to make folding screens, chairs, tables, chests, and beds. Zhejiang specializes in bamboo carvings of animals, both real and mythological: models are first constructed of bodiless lacquer over clay animal forms, then delicate threads of bamboo are plaited around the lacquer mold. A thin coat of lacquer is added as a final touch. The shapes of ancient bronzes and porcelains have also been gracefully adapted in woven bamboo. Pliable bamboo is truly the artisan's delight.

Delicate fan

FANS

Fans have been an important handicraft in China since the Tang dynasty. Flat fans of silk or paper were decorated with embroidery and painting: some of China's fine calligraphy and bird-and-flower paintings were done on silk fans. Folding fans made of sandalwood and bamboo were also popular. While noblemen purchased elaborately painted silk and carved fans of ivory and lacquer, villagers and farmers shopped for charming fans of gauze, feathers, woven bamboo, wheat straw, and dried grasses.

FOLK TOYS

Any inexpensive material was suitable for folk toys – clay, dough, cloth, straw, bamboo, and wood. Toys were often made by peasants for sale in the country market before traditional festivals. At the Mid-Autumn Festival in the middle of the eighth lunar month, for example, peddlars in Beijing sold clay models of the legendary three-legged hare that lived in the moon. There were all manner of these creatures, affectionately called "Gentlemen Hares," ranging in height from one to three feet. Warrior rabbits sported military dress with helmet and flag, while scholar rabbits wore gowns and carried umbrellas.

All types of folk toys are made today, and each region retains its traditional flavor. Shandong is famous for its papier-mâché lions and embroidered silk toys. Straw shoes in animal shapes with little faces on the toes give Chinese children toys to play with when they take their shoes off. Shaanxi is noted for its colorful terra-cotta whistles shaped as human figures, often characters from the local opera.

The craft of dough figures had its origin in the family kitchen, when a mother molded an extra bit of dough to become a toy for her child. In Beijing folk artists modeled miniature figures from dough and peddled them at markets or in the street. After kneading their colored dough, they rolled and shaped figures and added final touches with a scissor or comb. Opera characters, animals, and plump children were the subjects of this inexpensive craft. Some dough figures were even edible.

FOLK POTTERY AND FIGURINES

Folk potteries are often important crafts in communes in many parts of China, generally wherever good local clays are found. The pottery is produced during slack agricultural seasons and sold at the local market. Pots for bringing home live fish, food containers, and steamers are worked by hand using kickwheels.

Modeling small figurines of clay has also become an important folk specialty of certain regions. Wuxi is a traditional center for clay figures. Before 1949 folk artists sold their figures at temple fairs and local markets. Today this craft is studied in research centers, and more than two hundred types of figurines have been developed. They include children and characters from books, legends, and Chinese opera. Some pieces retain their folk character, while others are very sophisticated sculptures in the tradition of porcelain figures.

Kite making

KITES

The making of kites is an ancient handicraft that figures early in Chinese accounts. Kites were formed of paper with frames of lashed bamboo. When whistles were attached, the kites produced varying pitches in the wind. A spring sky covered with delicate and colorful kites must have been a lovely sight, as goldfish, butterfly, peacock, crane, and lion soared and danced in the

Hong-fu kite

breeze. In Beijing, autumn was the season for kite flying. Men and boys alike competed to create the most magnificent creatures, filling the sky with waving patterns of color. Today charming handpainted patterns of insects, birds, and animals decorate kites of all shapes. Although kite flying is now mainly a children's hobby in China, these ornamental crafts are still admired and carefully produced for sale all over the world.

REGIONAL CARVING

Village carvers used every available regional stone, as well as walnut shells, peach pits, bamboo, and local woods for carvings. The chrysanthemum stone found in Hunan Province has markings which resemble the flower in bud or full bloom, and carvers skillfully use the special markings of this stone in their designs. Qingtian soapstone carving has been a specialty of Wenzhou, Jiangsu Province, since the Tang dynasty. The stones, which occur in orange, cream, gray, and rainbow shades, are used not only for sculpture but for inlay work in screens and furniture. When polished, the stones take on a satin luster and resemble jade. Fuzhou carvers use a local softstone, Shoushan stone, with its fine, bright texture, to carve landscapes, animals, flowers, and human figures in the traditional style.

Bamboo carvers, with the traditional Chinese respect for the shape and texture of their materials, incorporate

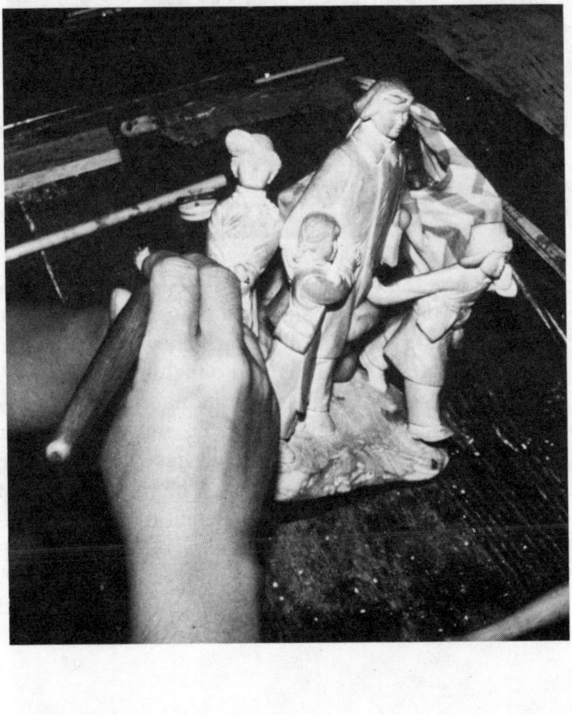

A regional carving

the natural contours of the joints into their designs. Polished relief sections make a striking contrast with the rough bamboo backgrounds in vases, boxes, and trays. Since the seventeenth century boxwood has been used in Zhejiang and Fujian provinces for fine furniture, screens, and architectural trim, as well as in folk sculpture. Hard, dense, and finely grained, the wood has a pale yellow tone which deepens and becomes more beautiful with age. Boxwood and boxwood root, as well as elm, azalea, and many other local woods are being used increasingly in contemporary carving.

Today's carvings combine traditional designs and motifs with modern themes from the everyday life of the people. Arts and crafts research institutes use regional stones and woods to carve expensive pieces for export, applying the time-honored techniques of jade and ivory carving. At the same time, carving has been taken up in small factory workshops throughout the country.

BATIK AND PEASANT PRINTS

Like folk arts the world over, Chinese folk textiles vary greatly in decoration and technique. Each village developed its own local style, which was further refined from family to family and daughter to daughter. In addition, each of China's minority nationalities, especially Zhuang, Yao, Miao, and Yi, has a particular decorative style and heritage which have increased the rich diversity of folk textile forms. The most important decorative techniques are hand stencil dyeing and embroidery. Colorful cross-stitch and satin stitch embroidery is mainly used on wedding crafts, although colorful embroidery decorates everyday clothing and household fabrics as well.

National minority costume

In addition to the practical value of textile work, this folk craft provided women with an artistic outlet; in fact, this was the only art form in which a woman of feudal China could take part. With her brilliant indigo dyes and bright threads, a peasant woman created something entirely her own, an expression of her personal taste and experience. The palace craftsman could not share this pleasure, as he designed an embroidery or tapestry within the rigid protocol of the court or according to the emperor's taste.

Cotton was introduced rather late in China and became widespread during the Song dynasty. While the nobility and the rich wore robes of fine silk, the great majority of Chinese wore homespun cotton decorated with natural indigo dyes. The old techniques are still used by village women today. For patterns, women use a waterproof stencil made from oiled paper or parchment. The open areas are covered with wax or a lime and soybean flour mixture, to resist the dye. The cloth is dipped in an indigo bath and then dried. Finally, the lime and flour paste is scraped off or the wax is boiled off. The fabric that emerges presents a bold contrast of creamy white and robust indigo. The cloth is used to make quilt covers, curtains, scarves, clothing, and even to wrap bundles. The minority women in China's south and southwest are especially noted for their bold batik pictures. The motifs they use are drawn from the lush life which surrounds them – birds in flight, coiling flowered vines, and skimming butterflies. Their pictures are often framed within striking geometric borders. These traditional designs are today copied for decoration in mass-produced textiles.

HANDICRAFTS SINCE 1950

Contemporary feather picture

Today all these age-old folk crafts are being researched, recorded, and preserved in craft institutes. In addition, new materials have been introduced, using basically the same techniques as those hundreds of years old. Since the 1950s shell carving has emerged in some coastal cities. Carved shells create landscapes and bird-and-flower paintings. The use of shells as a craft material is not entirely new, as tortoise shell and mother-of-pearl have traditionally been used for inlaying lacquer, ivory, and bronze. Craft workers today carefully choose shells for color, texture, pattern, and shape, and then carve and polish them to create a three-dimensional mosaic picture, usually in a traditional style. The mosaic is fashioned in such a way that the hidden colors, markings, and grain of the shells are integral to the final design. Other new materials now being used in regional crafts workshops are feathers, bark, and wheat and rice straw. Cuttlefish bone, water buffalo horn, coconut, and cork have also been added to the array of materials used by artisans in the craft revival of recent years.

Shell mosaic

FOR FURTHER READING

Chinese Papercuts. Hong Kong: John Warner Publications, 1978.

Ecke, Tseng Yu-ho. *Chinese Folk Art.* Honolulu: University Press of Hawaii, 1977.

Tun, Li-ch'en. *Annual Customs and Festivals in Peking.* Translated by Derk Bodde. Beijing: H. Vetch, 1936.

APPENDIX

GLOSSARY OF SPECIAL TERMS AND CHINESE CHARACTERS

An-hua	暗華	Secret decoration; incised decoration on ceramics
Bai dun-zi	白墩子	Petuntse, a white feldspathic clay used for making porcelain
Bi	璧	Circular shape with a central hole, frequently seen in carved jade
Chang	腸	Entrails; or endless knot motif
Cong	琮	A ritual jade shaped like a hollow tube within a square
Dan	丹	Cinnabar, the vermillion mercuric sulphide used by ancient Chinese alchemists
Die	耋	Seventy or eighty years old; elderly
Ding	鼎	Round bowl supported by three legs, dating back to the Neolithic period and later produced in bronze
Ding	定	Earliest known white porcelain ware
Dou-cai	鬥彩	Contrasting colors; polychrome porcelains decorated with underglaze blue and overglaze enamels
Fu	福	Symbol of prosperity
Fu-gui hua	富貴花	Flower of wealth and rank; peony
Guan	官	Official; the official ceramic wares of the Song dynasty
Guan-yin	觀音	Buddhist goddess of mercy
Gui guo yao	鬼國窑	Ware of the Devil's Country; an early description of cloisonné
He	荷	Lotus or water lily
He-ping	荷瓶	Lotus vase
He-ping	和平	Peace
Hong-fu	紅蝠	Red bat
Hong-fu	洪福	Abundant prosperity
Hu-die	蝴蝶	Butterfly
Jin-yu	金魚	Goldfish
Jin-yu	金余	Gold in abundance

Jun	鈞	An official stoneware of the Song dynasty
Ke-si	刻絲	Cut silk; a type of fine tapestry woven from silk
Lei-wen	雷文	Thunder motif, seen as early as the Neolithic period and still in use on crafts today
Li	鬲	Hollow-legged tripod cauldron, dating back to the Neolithic period and later produced in bronze
Lian	蓮	Lotus or water lily
Lian sheng gui zi	蓮笙桂子	Lotus, mouth pipe, cassia tree, and sons
Lian-sheng gui-zi	連生貴子	"May you give birth to sons who attain high rank for successive generations."
Ling-zhi	靈芝	Sacred fungus of immortality
Lu	鹿	Deer
Lu	祿	Official salary
Mei-ping	梅瓶	Plum vase; a ceramic vase for a single spray of plum blossoms
Men-hua	門畫	Door pictures; prints pasted on the doorway at the New Year
Men-shen	門神	Door guardians, popular subjects of New Year prints
Ming-qi	冥器	Tomb furnishings and figurines of clay, wood, and other materials
Nei-hua	內畫	Interior painting, a technique used especially in snuff bottles
Nian-hua	年畫	New Year pictures
Qilin	麒麟	Mythical composite creature, often called a unicorn
Qing	青	Nature in the growing phase; a spectrum of colors from green, blue, and gray to black
Ru	汝	An official stoneware of the Song dynasty
Ruan-yu	輭玉	Soft jade, or nephrite
San-cai	三彩	Three color; bold, polychrome, glazed ceramics of the Tang, or Ming porcelains with enamel glazes
Shan-shui	山水	Mountains and streams; landscape
Shou	壽	Symbol of longevity
Shu	蜀	Old term for the area of Sichuan
Shuang-xi	囍	Characters signifying "shared happiness," formed by placing two "happiness" symbols side by side
Temmoku	天目	Japanese term for a rich black Chinese stoneware, greatly admired in Japan

Wu-cai	五彩	Five color; polychrome porcelains decorated with underglaze blue and overglaze enamels
Xuan	宣	Fine absorbent paper used for painting or calligraphy
Yang	陽	Elements of nature considered to be male, such as brightness, dryness, and activity
Yang-cai	洋彩	Foreign colors; translucent enamels
Yang-ci	洋瓷	Foreign porcelain; painted enamelware
Yin	陰	Elements of nature considered to be female, such as darkness, wetness, and passivity
Ying-yu	硬玉	Hard jade, or jadeite
Yu	玉	Jade; a broad designation for many fine hardstones valued in China
Yue	粵	Old term for the area of Guangdong
Yue ware	越	Early green wares, fired at a high temperature
Zhen	鎮	Unwalled city
Zhen-yu	真玉	True jade, or nephrite
Zou-ma deng	走馬燈	Galloping horse lantern; a lantern which spun around due to the heat from a candle placed inside the lantern

SHOPPING FOR CRAFTS IN CHINA

There are a number of different types of outlets for Chinese products. Friendship Stores, which cater exclusively to foreign shoppers, are usually well stocked and carry an excellent variety of goods. There are Friendship Stores in all the major cities, the best ones in Beijing, Shanghai, and Guangzhou. If a city does not have a Friendship Store, one floor of a local department store is frequently set aside for visitors. Crafts kiosks or shops are now opening in all major tourist hotels and are often a good source of local products, as are small arts and crafts or antique shops. Factory outlets – small shops selling products produced in the local workshop – offer high quality products, while museum shops attached to major exhibition halls frequently carry superb reproductions and even originals in some cases. Foreign shoppers should be aware of the laws governing the export of antiques. True antiques are duty-free, but US duties on non-antique porcelains, bronzes, and jewelry can range from 25 to 100 percent, depending on the item. The formal requirement for imported antiques by US customs is a signed receipt from the dealer certifying that the item is more than one hundred and twenty years old.

POTTERY AND PORCELAIN

BEIJING

Shops specializing in fine porcelain can be found in all the major cities. In Beijing there is a good general ceramic shop at 99 Qianmen Street, and the shop at 149 Qianmen Street is devoted mainly to the porcelain of Jingdezhen. One of the best selections of old porcelains is available at 80 Liulichang Street in the Yunguzhai Beijing Antiquity Shop. The Cuizhenzhai Porcelain and Pottery Shop at 17 Liulichang Street has similar wares, while reproductions of Han and Tang tomb figurines are available at 137 Liulichang Street.

SHANGHAI AND GUANGZHOU

In Shanghai, porcelains are found at the Ceramics Store, 550 Nanjing Road; the Chuanxin Shop, 1297

Huaihai Road; and the Number One Department Store. The antique shop at 694 Nanjing Road is also worth investigating. Finally, the shop attached to the Shanghai Museum of Art and History carries excellent reproductions of Tang figurines from the museum collection. The Guangzhou Antique Shop on Wende Road in Guangzhou is also renowned for its collection of old porcelain.

PROVINCIAL CENTERS

In provinces where major kilns are located, the capital cities often have exhibition halls featuring the finest porcelains and pottery in the region; small retail outlets are often attached. Nanchang, in Jiangxi Province, has an exhibition hall featuring the wares of Jingdezhen; Changsha, capital of Hunan Province, features porcelain from Liling and other Hunan kilns. There are a number of large ceramics shops in both of these cities which carry a varied and interesting selection of modern novelty ceramics and fine new porcelains. These cities also have some interesting antique shops where a selection of old wares may be found, including snuff bottles, rouge cases, small vases, and so forth.

The Shiwan Ceramic Arts Factory in Guangdong Province has a small shop which sells charming glazed or unglazed miniature figurines. It is well worth a visit to this kiln just to observe the techniques involved in the production of these small sculptures. Ceramic workshops which make reproductions of Tang *san-cai* tomb figures are located in Xian, Nanjing, and Luoyang; many of these workshops have retail outlets. Pottery and porcelain research centers and arts and crafts research institutes are also good sources for glazed, enameled, and engraved porcelains.

JADE, HARDSTONES, AND IVORY

BEIJING, SHANGHAI, AND GUANGZHOU

The finest selection of jade and hardstone carvings and jewelry is found in the stores of Beijing and Shanghai; the Guangzhou Friendship Store has excellent ivory carvings, not found elsewhere in the city. In Beijing the Yunguzhai Jade Shop at 108 Liulichang Street carries old and modern jade carvings, such as snuff bottles and other small pieces. At 70 Liulichang, in the Beijing Antiquities Shop, shoppers will find antique hardstone jewelry and some fine old ivory pieces. There is a jewelry shop at 229 Wangfujing Street, and the second floor of the Arts and Crafts Store at 200 Wangfujing is worth investigating. In Shanghai be sure to go to the Number One Department Store and the Antique Shop at 694 Nanjing Road for both old and new carvings. The Guangzhou Antique Shop on Wende Road, actually a collection of small shops catering to foreigners, has a helpful staff who will be glad to show you old jades. A shop called the Decorative Ornaments and Housewares Stores, at 393 Zhongshan Road, also carries jades. There are a number of jade carving studios in these cities.

PROVINCIAL CENTERS

Workshops in Zhengzhou, Nanjing, Yangzhou, and Suzhou, all located in eastern China, specialize in fine hardstone carving. Tianjin, Xian, Shenyang, and Harbin, in northern China, now have jade and ivory carving workshops and produce some fine products which are sold in their retail outlets.

SILK WEAVING AND EMBROIDERY

BEIJING, SHANGHAI, AND GUANGZHOU

Silks and embroideries are good buys in China, and in general the selection of patterns is excellent. Some old brocades and theatrical costumes may be found in Beijing in the Arts and Crafts Trust Company at 12 Dongdan Street. Shanghai has a silk yardage store on 592 Nanjing Road, and a good selection of embroidery is available at the Friendship Stores in both Shanghai and Guangzhou.

SUZHOU

Suzhou, in Jiangsu Province, is the center for silk embroidery; the National Embroidery Institute and the Suzhou Institute of Embroidery are both located here. Guests may watch artisans making double-sided embroidery and purchase fine quality art works or inexpensive items here. *Ke-si* tapestries are also made here.

HANGZHOU AND OTHER PROVINCIAL CENTERS

Hangzhou, in Zhejiang Province, is the center of the huge Hangzhou Silk Dyeing Mill, where visitors can watch the whole process of creating silk. Woven brocade pictures are a specialty of the Hangzhou Brocade Factory; favorite themes include West Lake and the surrounding countryside. Silks are readily available by the yard, and there is an abundant selection of embroidery and clothing in the department stores and silk shops of Wuxi, as well as in Suzhou and Hangzhou.

Changsha, in Hunan Province, has a fine embroidery workshop where pieces made in the shop are on exhibition. Embroidered landscapes, double-sided embroideries, and other excellent quality pieces are for sale.

Chengdu, in Sichuan Province, is an old center for silk and has a fine arts and crafts store where the local specialty – embroidered silk squares – is sold.

LACQUERWARE

BEIJING, SHANGHAI, AND GUANGZHOU

The Friendship Stores in Beijing, Shanghai, and Guangzhou are all well stocked with lacquerware, as are the hotel boutiques in these cities. Beautifully carved vases, cosmetic boxes, plates, jars, and lacquerware trays inlaid with mother-of-pearl are all readily available. In Beijing the Arts and Crafts Store at 200 Wangfujing and the Arts and Crafts Trust Company at 12 Dongdan Street both carry fine lacquerware. The floor devoted to arts and crafts in the Number One Department Store in Shanghai also has a good selection of carved, inlaid, and bodiless lacquerware. The Hall of Arts and Crafts in Haizhu Square, Guangzhou, features many crafts in its exhibition hall and has a large store on the ground floor. The Chuanxin Shop at 1297 Huaihai Road is also worth a visit.

PROVINCIAL CENTERS

Chengdu and Chongqing in Sichuan Province have a fine selection of lacquerware, reflecting the two thousand-year-old history of this art in the region. Visitors may watch the lacquerware being produced at a workshop in Chongqing; a retail outlet is attached. Other craft centers include Nanning, Yangzhou, Suzhou, and Changsha. Fuzhou also specializes in bodiless lacquerware–there are at least two studios producing lacquer in this city, and both have retail outlets attached.

CLOISONNE, METALWORK, AND GLASS

BEIJING, SHANGHAI, AND GUANGZHOU

The best selection of fine cloisonné vases, boxes, and jewelry, as well as reproductions of ancient bronzes and gold and silver filigree jewelry, will be found in the Friendship Stores in Beijing, Shanghai, and Guangzhou. Cloisonné is a specialty of Beijing, which has arts and crafts workshops where visitors can see these fine enamelwares being produced; outlet shops are usually attached to these craft shops. The arts and crafts store at 200 Wangfujing Street carries cloisonné and jewelry on the second floor. The jewelry store at 299 Wangfujing has fine pieces with inlaid precious stones. The Beijing Antiquities Shop at 70 Liulichang Street has some fine old cloisonné. Bronze reproductions of ancient ritual vessels may be purchased at 64 Liulichang Street, as well as at the shops attached to the Museum of Chinese History in Beijing and the Museum of Art and History in Shanghai. Old pieces of cloisonné and enamelware

are available at the Shanghai Antique Shop at 694 Nanjing Road; in Guangzhou, these may be found at the Guangzhou Antique Shop on Wende Road, and at 393 Zhongshan Road.

PROVINCIAL CENTERS

Gold and silver jewelry and small decorative pieces are made in the workshops of Suzhou. Filigree jewelry is a specialty of both Chengdu and Chongqing, in Sichuan Province. The Friendship Stores and local arts and crafts stores are good shopping spots in these areas.

FOLK AND REGIONAL ARTS

BEIJING, SHANGHAI, AND GUANGZHOU

Friendship Stores feature folk arts from every region of China – bamboo carving, wheat straw pictures, papercuts, and all kinds of local wood and stone carvings. While these are all available in the main centers, certain folk arts are best purchased in the region where they are made. In Beijing, at 200 Wangfujing Street, local products and folk crafts from all over the country are available, including batiks from Yunnan, fans, baskets, and bamboo wares. In Shanghai the Number One Department Store and the Papercut Store at 751 Nanjing Road have a selection of folk crafts, including a large variety of intricate papercuts from every region. A rich selection of regional crafts is available for purchase at the Shanghai Arts and Crafts Research Institute. In Guangzhou, at 65 Renmin Road, there is a lantern shop, where intricate lanterns of wood, paper, and silk may be purchased; many of these are collapsible for easy packing. The Hall of Arts and Crafts in Haizhu Square has a large selection of sandalwood fans, bamboo carvings, woven baskets, and other crafts.

THE EASTERN REGION

Jiangsu and Zhejiang provinces are famous for their great variety of handicrafts. In addition to being silk weaving and embroidery centers, Suzhou, Hangzhou, and Nanjing feature fine lanterns, fans of antique silk, bamboo, and sandalwood; woven straw products; painted eggs; papercuts; woodcuts; and silk flowers. Wuxi, which is also a silk center, produces clay figurines in the Huishan Clay Figure Workshop, which has a small retail outlet. Jinan in Shandong has a marvelous selection of straw and bamboo products.

THE NORTHERN REGION

The area has recently started new craft workshops; since the 1950s seashell mosaics, feather pictures, wheat straw mosaics, and oxhorn carvings have been developed as regional crafts. Shenyang, Harbin, Qinhuangdao, and Dalian are centers for these products. Tianjin is noted for its fine carpets. Folk crafts include kites, bamboo products, and New Year's pictures from nearby Weifang. A terra-cotta ceramics factory makes small figures that may be bought at the retail shop attached.

THE SOUTHERN REGION

Foshan, near Guangzhou, is a center for the development of regional folk arts. An arts and crafts research institute is located here. Lanterns, carved bamboo, and papercuts of extremely high quality are produced and sold in the attached retail shop. Changsha features regional handicrafts ranging from local pottery and embroidery to shell crafts and baskets. Fuzhou crafts include local stone carvings, pottery, and lovely woven bamboo products. Nanchang features the fine folk crafts of Jiangxi Province—pottery of all kinds, and lacquered woven baskets in lovely animal shapes.

THE SOUTHWEST

Guilin, Nanning, and Kunming are the heart of the Zhuang, Miao, Yao, and Shui nationalities districts. The crafts of this region include superb batiks; colorful weavings of handbags, quilts, and tablecloths; embroideries for use as pillow covers and skirts; and so forth. Arts and crafts stores in these cities are well worth a special trip. Nanning has a research institute where varied local crafts are made, including bamboo ware, textiles, wood carving, pottery, and lacquerware. Kunming's Store of the Nationalities has colorful hats, skirts, and blankets.

THE CENTRAL REGION

In Xian, Luoyang, Wuhan, and Datong regional pottery is a major specialty. Lanterns, bamboo ware, local stone and wood carvings, and papercuts are found in the local arts and crafts shops or department stores.

THE WESTERN REGION

Sichuan has been a famous craft center for centuries. Regional lacquerware, embroidery, and gold and silver filigree work are famous throughout China, but Sichuan is also known for its folk arts. Lanterns in the shape of birds and animals, local pottery, and woven straw and bamboo are found the local stores of Chongqing and Chengdu.

INDEX

CREDITS

Rewi Alley, pp. 98, 101, 103 (top), 111, 115 (top)
Brooklyn Museum, gift of Stanley J. Love, p. 153 (top); gift of Samuel P. Avery, p. 158
China National Arts and Crafts Import and Export Corporation (Beijing), pp. 37, 118, and all color plates
China Photo Service, p. 162 (right)
Joseph A. Cohen, pp. 119 (left), 178, 179 (right), 186 (top)
Dover Publications, Inc., pp. 41, 123 (bottom), 124
Sharon Hare, pp. 22, 103, 105, 174, 177
Metropolitan Museum of Art, pp. 108, 140, 141, 142
William Rockhill Nelson Gallery of Art, pp. 8, 30-31, 100, 104, 121, 143, 150, 151, 155, 162
James Nesi, pp. 99 (top), 105, 132, 147, 149 (top), 165, 166, 167
New York Public Library, Prints Division, Astor, Lenox and Tilden Foundations, pp. 38, 82, 138
Rosalind Rose, pp. 128, 129, 130, 131, 132, 183
Katherine Smalley, frontispiece, p. 133
Xinhua News Agency, pp. 7, 9, 14, 17, 19, 20, 21, 23, 25, 35, 83, 88, 90, 92, 93, 96, 97, 98, 99 (bottom), 106, 109, 115, 116, 117, 123, 127, 133, 134, 139, 149, 155, 157, 160, 163, 164, 179, 181, 185, 186
The authors, pp. 46, 58 (top), 62 (top), 74, 76 (top), 78 (bottom), 86, 120, 135, 179 (left)
Line drawings by Mr. Chu Chen-kuang, pp. 43, 45, 47, 50, 51, 58 (bottom), 64 (top), 77 (top), 86
Line drawings by Frank Fontana, pp. 40, 89, 90, 91, 95, 98, 116, 124, 151, 152, 180, 182
Line drawings by Susan Lutsky, pp. 48, 61, 107